Optimizing Career Engagement

Optimizing Career Engagement

A GUIDE FOR ENHANCING CAREERS AND OTHER LIFE ROLES

Deirdre A. Pickerell and Roberta A. Borgen

cognella®
SAN DIEGO

Bassim Hamadeh, CEO and Publisher
Amy Smith, Senior Project Editor
Rachel Kahn, Production Editor
Emely Villavicencio, Senior Graphic Designer
Kylie Bartolome, Licensing Associate/Coordinator
Natalie Piccotti, Director of Marketing
Kassie Graves, Senior Vice President, Editorial
Jamie Giganti, Director of Academic Publishing

Cover images:
Copyright © 2019 iStockphoto LP/sarayut.
Copyright © 2020 iStockphoto LP/Alena Butusava.

Printed in the United States of America.

cognella® | ACADEMIC PUBLISHING
3970 Sorrento Valley Blvd., Ste. 500, San Diego, CA 92121

BRIEF CONTENTS

Preface xiii

Part I: Career Engagement: Context, Model, and Research 1

1   The Context 3

2   The Career Engagement Model 11

3   Challenge: Motivating Work 21

4   Challenge: Meaningful Opportunities 33

5   Capacity: Resources 43

6   Capacity: Relationships 51

7   Capacity: Workload 65

8   Capacity: Well-Being 75

9   Capacity: Fit 85

Part II: Working With Career Engagement 95

10 Career Engagement for Individuals 97

11 Career Engagement for Managers, Supervisors,
    and Coaches 107

12 Career Engagement for Leaders and Policymakers 123

Part III: Beyond Career Engagement: Living Life to the Fullest.. 137

13   Student Engagement... 139

14   Family Engagement... 149

15   Community Engagement 157

16   Retirement Engagement 165

17   Staying Engaged Across All Life Roles 175

Index 183

DETAILED CONTENTS

Preface xiii

Part I: Career Engagement: Context, Model, and Research 1

1   The Context 3
     Changing Contexts 3
     Activities 5
         1.1 Current Context: A Reflection..5
         1.2 What's Working? What's Not? 6
     Five Big Ideas 7
     References 8

2   The Career Engagement Model.. 11
     Exploring Career Engagement 11
     Employee/Work Engagement 11
     Flow Theory 13
     Career Engagement 13
     Applying Career Engagement 17
     Activities 17
         2.1 Level of Engagement 17
     Five Big Ideas 19
     References 19

3   Challenge: Motivating Work.. 21
     Exploring the Factor: Motivating Work 21
     Applying Career Engagement 23
     Activities 24
         3.1 Unpacking Motivation.. 24
         3.2 Intrinsic versus Extrinsic Motivation 27
     Five Big Ideas 30
     References 31

4   Challenge: Meaningful Opportunities.. 33
     Exploring the Factor: Meaningful Opportunities 33
     Applying Career Engagement 35
     Activities 37
         4.1 Meaningful Opportunities... 37

4.2 Know Your Why! 37

4.3 Finding Your 5Ps: Pride, Passion, Purpose, Performance, and Poise 39

Five Big Ideas 40

References 41

5   **Capacity: Resources** 43

Exploring the Factor: Resources 44

Applying Career Engagement 45

Activities 46

5.1 Resource Mapping: Taking Stock 46

5.2 Weekly Life/Role Priorities 48

Five Big Ideas 50

References 50

6   **Capacity: Relationships** 51

Exploring the Factor: Relationships 52

Applying Career Engagement 54

Activities 55

6.1 Relationships Matter 55

6.2 Synergy: When Two Are Stronger Than One 59

6.3 When You Hurt, I Hurt: Vicarious Trauma 61

Five Big Ideas 62

References 62

7   **Capacity: Workload** 65

Exploring the Factor: Workload 65

Applying Career Engagement 67

Activities 68

7.1 Jar of Rocks 68

7.2 Managing Time and Tasks 70

Five Big Ideas 71

References 72

8   **Capacity: Well-Being** 75

Exploring the Factor: Well-Being 75

Applying Career Engagement 76

Activities 78

8.1 Balance Wheel 78

8.2 What's Working? What's Not? 79

8.3 Journaling 81

Five Big Ideas 83

References 84

9   **Capacity: Fit** 85

Exploring the Factor: Fit 86

Applying Career Engagement 86

Activities 87

    9.1 Culture Audits 87

    9.2 Values Checklist 91

Five Big Ideas 92

References 93

Part II: Working With Career Engagement 95

10   Career Engagement for Individuals 97

Exploring Career Engagement for Individuals 98

Applying Career Engagement 98

Activities 99

    10.1 Monitor Your Career Engagement 99

    10.2 What's Working? What's Not? 100

    10.3 Know Yourself 102

    10.4 Explore Opportunities 102

    10.5 Identify a Starting Point 103

    10.6 Avoid Disengagement 105

Five Big Ideas 105

References 106

11   Career Engagement for Managers, Supervisors,
and Coaches 107

Exploring Career Engagement for Managers, Supervisors, and Coaches 108

Applying Career Engagement 109

Activities 110

    11.1 Motivating Projects and Meaningful Opportunities 110

    11.2 Key Influencers 111

    11.3 Provide Relevant Resources 113

    11.4 Strengthen Relationships 114

    11.5 Critically Assess Workload 115

    11.6 Facilitate Health and Wellness 116

    11.7 Recognize the Importance of Fit 117

    11.8 Align Challenge and Capacity 118

Five Big Ideas 120

References 121

12   Career Engagement for Leaders and Policymakers 123

Exploring Career Engagement for Leaders and Policymakers 124

Applying Career Engagement 125

Activities 126

    12.1 Understand Career/Life Engagement 126

    12.2 Look for Synergies 127

12.3 Establish a Baseline 129

12.4 Equip Leaders 131

12.5 Recognize Limits to Capacity 131

12.6 Look for Challenge Opportunities 132

12.7 Watch for Disengagement 133

12.8 Communicate the Benefits 133

Five Big Ideas 134

References 135

Part III: Beyond Career Engagement: Living Life to the Fullest

.... 137

13   Student Engagement 139

Exploring Student Engagement 139

Applying Career Engagement 141

Activities 141

13.1 How Did We Do Today? 141

13.2 This Week Went 144

Five Big Ideas 147

References 148

14   Family Engagement 149

Exploring Family Engagement 149

Applying Career Engagement 151

Activities 152

14.1   Family Visioning 152

14.2   Asset Mapping 154

Five Big Ideas 155

References 155

15   Community Engagement 157

Exploring Community Engagement 157

Applying Career Engagement 159

Activities 160

15.1 Mapping Community Resources 160

15.2 Getting to Know You 161

Five Big Ideas 163

References 164

16.   Retirement Engagement 165

Exploring Retirement Engagement 165

Applying Career Engagement 167

Activities 168

16.1 Six Circles of Life 168

16.2 Retirement Activities Checklist 170

Five Big Ideas 173

References 174

17   Staying Engaged Across All Life Roles 175

Activities 180

   17.1 What's Working? What's Not? A Life Role Inventory 180

   17.2 Optimizing Engagement Across All Life Roles 181

Big Ideas 181

References 182

Index 183

PREFACE

W ELCOME TO THE world of career engagement, a model we developed in 2011 after decades of work in career development practice and leadership and in management/corporate consulting, with a focus on topics such as recruitment, retention, outplacement, and engagement. Despite immersion in these two separate fields of inquiry and practice, the career engagement model emerged because nothing else seemed to fit well enough. This book outlines the history and development of the career engagement model, along with our current thinking on how it fits within the broader conversation around work and life engagement.

In every chapter, we open with a case vignette—a story of an individual, couple, or family and how the chapter's focused content applies. In Chapter 1, this content is focused on the changing world of work—an important backdrop, especially in light of the COVID-19 pandemic that ravaged the world starting in late 2019 and continuing for the following years. The context in the remaining chapters focuses on various elements of the career engagement model. First, in Chapter 2, we look at career engagement overall. Chapters 3–9 explore the factors that contribute to career engagement: motivating work, meaningful opportunities, resources, relationships, workload, well-being, and fit. Chapters 10–17 look at the model in specific contexts, starting with individuals striving to optimize engagement and managers/supervisors, along with leaders and policymakers, supporting engagement. The remaining chapters focus on career engagement for students, families, communities, and retirees and end with staying engaged across all life roles.

Each chapter applies the career engagement content to the case vignette, bringing to life the real-world application of the model. Activities and exercises are shared throughout, first applied to the vignette, followed by space and prompts for individuals to engage in personal reflection. We have used many of these activities in our practice, both with individual clients and within organizations, and we hope they help you optimize career engagement in your life. Some of the activities have been adapted from previous publications, most notably *Career Strategies for a Lifetime of Success* (3rd ed.), written by Dr. Roberta Neault (now Borgen) in 2012.

To end each chapter, we present five big ideas. With these, we summarize the chapter's key points to remember. These are the tips/strategies we believe are most important in helping you understand and experience career engagement across life roles.

Each chapter has a reference list where you can explore various topics in further detail. Our previous academic work and publications[1] provide a more in-depth review of the development of the model and the body of work that influenced its development.

Our goal with this guide is to provide sufficient information to explain the model and how it fits within important conversations about work and life. Ultimately, however, this is intended to be a guide or workbook that equips readers and stakeholders to use the model.

---

1   It's important to note that publications attributed to Roberta Neault were all written by the second author of this book, Roberta Borgen, whose name changed with her marriage in 2020. Mid-career name changes can be challenging for professionals, especially authors, but represent the inextricable interconnectedness of our many life roles!

PART I

Career Engagement: Context, Model, and Research

CHAPTER ONE

The Context

IMG. 1.1

The Gill family could never have envisioned the changes they were to experience in the spring of 2020, after the World Health Organization confirmed that COVID-19 had officially become a global pandemic. Prior to spring break they were living what they had come to take for granted as a "normal" life. Channan and her husband, Hardeep, were both working full-time in professional jobs—Channan as an accountant and Hardeep as a university professor. Their three children, Jas (15), Raj (12), and Sukhi (9) were doing well in school, and each of them were engaged in out-of-school activities: school and community sports, dance, and Punjabi classes. As a family they also attended programs and festivals at the Gurdwara (the Sikh temple in their community). They lived in a comfortable, large home in the suburbs, sharing the home with Hardeep's parents and an unmarried uncle, Paatav, who was studying engineering at the local university. In all, eight of them lived together in their house.

Then, almost overnight, they were all working and studying from home—all day, every day! After-school activities were suspended, universities shifted to e-learning, and, right in the midst of the busy tax season, all of the accountants in Channan's office were told to work from home. A bit later, even the Gurdwara was closed. The grandparents, not used to having company at home with them during the day, saw this as bonus time with the family. They wandered through the house, stopping to chat with each person individually, apparently oblivious to whether someone was in a Zoom meeting or studying for an exam.

Changing Contexts

Likely every generation has both celebrated and cursed society's advances. Splitting the atom gave glimpses into the origins of the universe and the potential for endless power while also allowing for the creation of perhaps humankind's most destructive force (Amadeo, 2020). Readily available antibiotics cured illness, but overuse has given rise to "super bugs" that can overrun the medical profession (Weledjia et al., 2017). Technological advances such as the internet and cell phones allow for incredible opportunities for work and play, seemingly making the world smaller and more connected (Blustein, 2019), yet concurrently bringing pressure to be endlessly online, increased potential for vision problems and musculoskeletal disorders, and higher rates of anxiety (Lagudu, 2021).

The notion of work has also advanced and evolved over the past several generations. In the mid 20th century, *work* most often referred to paid employment that was, at least in some communities and cultures, entirely separate from other aspects of one's life. Once an occupational choice was made, there may have been limited opportunity for change; in these times many workers had only one employer for their whole career. Today, career is considered much more broadly. The European Lifelong Guidance Partnership Network defined career as "the interaction of work roles and other life roles over a person's lifespan, including how they balance paid and unpaid work, and their involvement in learning and education" (Jackson, 2012, p. 11).

That work is now seen as more than a paid job is likely an advancement that should be celebrated. Certainly, increased choice and flexibility and acknowledgement of other life roles, and how they intersect, are all positive outcomes. However, for some there has been an eroding of the employment contract, resulting in precarious work and income inequality and the importance of considering a universal basic income (Blustein, 2019; Zizys, 2014). Global mobility and increasing cultural diversity in the workplace has, for many, expanded work opportunities. On the other hand, access to global markets isn't always positive (Zhang, 2019) and racial discrimination in the workplace is at an all-time high (Gurchiek, 2020). Perhaps spurred by the youth of today's demand for action on a variety of social issues (e.g., climate change, gender/racial inequality; Liao, 2020) or through initiatives such as the United Nation's (n.d.) Sustainable Development Goals, others are looking at ways their work and lives can contribute to a greater good.

What seems quite clear is that the world of work has undergone some massive transformations over the last few decades, and these changes seem to be increasing at an exponential rate. As a result, individuals may make multiple work transitions over the course of a lifetime (Blustein, 2019; Kasriel, 2016, Pickerell & Neault, 2019). Navigating these changes, however, is not always easy, especially given the rapid pace of change, coupled with the importance work has on factors including mental health and well-being, identity, and family (Blustein, 2019; Redekopp & Huston, 2020).

And the massive transformations continue, sometimes quite dramatically and unexpectedly. The entire Gill family, in the opening vignette, was impacted when COVID-19 was declared a global pandemic. In truth, almost every family, across every country, was impacted, and the numbers are shocking. At one point in spring 2022, the World Health Organization (WHO, 2022) reported 483,556,595 confirmed cases and 6,132,461 deaths.

By mid pandemic, over 220 million jobs were lost globally (Larson, 2021) and "tens of millions of people are at risk of falling into extreme poverty ... [and] nearly half of the world's 3.3 billion global workforce are at risk of losing their livelihoods" (WHO, 2020, paras. 1, 2).

Among the many life lessons from the COVID-19 pandemic is that we need to be prepared for big shifts in our careers and other life roles. Although career planning is important, and can definitely be helpful, plans can be disrupted, economies change, and individuals need the resiliency to adapt and to engage in lifelong career decision-making.

In our vignette, everyone in the Gill family was impacted by pandemic-related changes. Channan had to carve out space in her very busy home for processing confidential tax returns for her clients, without access to her support staff, copying equipment, or multiple computer screens. Concurrently, Hardeep, in his role as a university professor, along with his brother, Paatav, a university student, had to adjust to teaching and learning online. They were all in Zoom meetings for hours each day, competing for use of the one private home office with the most stable internet access and the best camera and sound on the computer. Everyone who lost the competition resorted to working from various laptop computers, tablets, and smartphones in whatever quiet corner of the house they could find. Sometimes, with multiple Zoom meetings going on, the floor of the walk-in closet in Channan and Hardeep's bedroom offered the most private option.

Hardeep, because of his more flexible schedule as a professor, and also because of his teaching expertise, had to take on an additional role of homeschooling their three children and also tutoring his brother who began to struggle a bit in his university courses without in-person access to his instructors, teaching assistants, and classmates. Although he loved teaching, Hardeep didn't love teaching subjects that were less familiar to him—and he especially didn't like the arguments with his children about "that's not the way the teacher said to do it!"

As individual roles and responsibilities shift, in the midst of bigger changes within unique regional, cultural, and economic contexts, life and career satisfaction can be impacted. The career engagement model, introduced in the next chapter and expanded upon throughout the book, provides a conceptual framework for understanding the interconnectedness of individual and contextual characteristics and how they impact one's feelings of being bored, burned out, or fully engaged.

Activities

1.1   Current Context: A Reflection

Context is often important when considering opportunities to feel engaged and fulfilled within work and other life roles. In the example that follows, Channan took a moment to reflect on how the COVID-19 pandemic has impacted her over the past several months.

Wow! We are about 10 months into the COVID-19 pandemic and I'm not 100% sure how I feel. At first, life was completely overwhelming. We have a large home, and treasure our interconnected family, but everyone home at once, needing to use the internet and private spaces to do work and school was difficult. We kept tripping over each other! We then settled into a routine that seemed to work. Lately, however, I think we are just all tired—tired of the restrictions, tired of shifting goal posts, and tired of each other! I adore my family, but always being together is challenging. At the same time, I'm very aware that we've had quite a different experience from our family in India, and in many regions around the world. Do I really have a "right" to complain?

Now it's your turn.

1.2   What's Working? What's Not?

It can also be helpful to focus on specific life roles, or circumstances, reflecting on what is working well and what isn't. In these reflections (adapted from Neault, 2012), it is okay if everything, or nothing, is working. Step 1 is to identify, then to plan around where change may be needed. Here is what Channan did.

	What's Working?	What's Not?
At Home	Everyone is home for dinner, every night. We feel more connected, rather than "ships passing."	The longer we are on lockdown, the more it feels like we are always on top of each other.
At Work	It is busy, but everything is going well. My employer has been incredibly supportive!	
In My Relationships	We've established a good routine for work, school, and family time.	The children are really struggling, especially Sukhi.
In My Community	Temple has done an amazing job transitioning food service outside.	Virtual services are not the same!

Now it's your turn.

	What's Working?	What's Not?
At Home		
At Work		
In My Relationships		
In My Community		
Other		

Adapted from Roberta Neault, *Career Strategies for a Lifetime of Success*. Copyright © 2012 by Life Strategies Ltd. Reprinted with permission.

Five Big Ideas

1. **Career is lifelong.** Not all that long ago, the term *career* was linked to a professional vocational identity (e.g., lawyer, nurse, dentist), and it represented the work one did for money. Now, however, career is used much more broadly to represent a compilation of paid and unpaid work, along with learning and leisure activities, across a life span. With this definition, everyone has a career (i.e., not just professionals), and there are useful career development activities for children in grade school right through to retirees.

2. **Career is a personal experience.** Regardless of how similar careers may seem on the surface, each person's career journey will be unique. Where you live, your individual identities, your access to supports, and numerous other factors will create a life story, and therefore a career story, like no other.

3. **Life is ever-changing.** Today's society is in constant flux. Advances in technology, catastrophic events, global pandemics, and changes in government mean that your work, and your lives, are never static, even when daily routines seem monotonous. Recognizing that societal forces, even halfway around the world, have far-reaching impacts can help you be better prepared for, or less shocked by, inevitable shifts.

4. **Career development and mental health are inextricably linked.** Engaging in career development processes and practices and doing work that fits with your unique self can improve mental health outcomes. Different from mental *illness*, mental health relates to stress, coping, anxiety, and well-being.

5. **Every person deserves an opportunity to be in work that allows them to thrive.** Although where you live and what you do can make a massive difference, most people will spend about one third of their lives at work (Giattino et al., 2013). It makes sense, therefore, that this work should be safe, where you are able to bring your best self, make use of your unique talents, and have a sense of fit and belonging.

References

Amadeo, K. (2020, November). *Nuclear power in America, how it works, pros, cons, and its impact: Is nuclear power the answer to climate change?* The Balance. https://www.thebalance.com/nuclear-power-how-it-works-pros-cons-impact-3306336

Blustein, D. L. (2019). *The importance of work in an age of uncertainty. The eroding work experience in America.* Oxford University Press.

Giattino, C., Ortiz-Ospina, E., & Roser, M. (2013). *Working hours.* https://ourworldindata.org/working-hours

Gurchiek, K. (2020, July 8). *Employees look to employer to rise up against racism.* SHRM. https://www.shrm.org/ResourcesAndTools/hr-topics/behavioral-competencies/global-and-cultural-effectiveness/Pages/Employees-Look-to-Employers-to-Rise-Up-Against-Racism.aspx

Jackson, C. (Ed.). (2012). *The European Lifelong Guidance Partnership Network (ELGPN) glossary.* European Lifelong Guidance Partnership Network. http://www.elgpn.eu/publications/browse-by-language/english/elgpn-tools-no.-2-llg-glossary/

Kasriel, S. (2016, November 13). *By 2030, will we all be our own boss?* World Economic Forum. www.weforum.org/agenda/2016/11/by-2030-will-we-all-be-our-own-boss/

Lagudu, S. (2021, November 30). *10 harmful side effects of mobile phones on teenagers.* Mom Junction. https://www.momjunction.com/articles/side-effects-of-mobile-phones-on-teenagers_00352682/

Larson, N. (2021, January 25). *225 million jobs were lost worldwide in 2020 thanks to the pandemic, report finds*. CTV. https://www.ctvnews.ca/health/coronavirus/225-million-jobs-were-lost-worldwide-in-2020-thanks-to-the-pandemic-report-finds-1.5281152

Liao, K. (2020, December 23). *6 ways young people stepped up to make the world a better place in 2020*. Global Citizen. https://www.globalcitizen.org/en/content/2020-youth-activism/

Neault, R. (2012). *Career strategies for a lifetime of success* (3rd ed.). Life Strategies.

Pickerell, D. A., & Neault, R. A. (2019). Maximizing career engagement across a lifetime of transitions. In J. G. Maree (Ed.) *Handbook of innovative career counselling* (pp. 195–211). Springer Nature.

Redekopp, D. E., & Huston, M. (2020). *Strengthening mental health through effective career development: A practitioner's guide*. CERIC.

United Nations (n.d.). *Sustainable development goals*. https://sdgs.un.org/goals

Weledji, E. P., Weledji, E. K., Assob, J. C., & Nsagha, D. S. (2017). Pros, cons and future of antibiotics. *New Horizons in Translational Medicine, 4,* 9–14. https://www.researchgate.net/publication/322012425_Pros_Cons_and_future_of_antibiotics

World Health Organization. (2020, October). *Impact of COVID-19 on people's livelihoods, their health and our food systems*. https://www.who.int/news/item/13-10-2020-impact-of-covid-19-on-people's-livelihoods-their-health-and-our-food-systems

World Health Organization. (2021). *WHO coronavirus (COVID-19) dashboard*. https://covid19.who.int/

Zhang, J. (2019, July 3). *Global brain circulation: The gift of global talent*. Alariss Insights. https://alariss.com/global-brain-circulation/

Zizys, T. (2014). *Better work: The path to good jobs is through employers*. Metcalf Foundation. https://metcalffoundation.com/wp-content/uploads/2014/10/2014-10-02-Better-Work.pdf

Figure Credit

IMG 1.1: Copyright © 2013 Depositphotos/monkeybusiness.

CHAPTER TWO

The Career Engagement Model

IMG. 2.1

Tom loved his life! Just last year, he'd won the top award in his department for his innovative solution to a longstanding logistics problem. Financially, he was in the best place he'd ever been; a recent meeting with his financial advisor confirmed that he was on track to retire comfortably in 5 years. Last year he had remarried, and their blended family and 3-month-old baby brought delight to his life every day.

Then, completely unexpectedly, a meeting with his manager that Tom had fully expected to be about a salary increase resulted instead in a layoff notice due to corporate restructuring. "Nothing personal," the manager tried to assure Tom, but it definitely felt personal, and it impacted absolutely every part of Tom's life!

Exploring Career Engagement

To fully understand the career engagement model, it's important to explore and acknowledge the bodies of work that influenced our thinking and what factors inspired us to go in a new direction. To begin, we present a brief overview of employee/work engagement and flow theory and how our work emerged, and then separated, from these avenues of thought. This helps situate our work in the broader conversations but is, by no means, intended to be an in-depth review of the literature of the time. For that, we invite readers to explore our previous work and the sources cited throughout this book.

Employee/Work Engagement

The concept of *engagement* within the workplace (e.g., job engagement, employee engagement) was first introduced by William Kahn in 1990. Long considered the father of employee engagement, Kahn's *need-satisfying approach* focused on the workers' ability to bring their full selves to work. To ensure this was possible, Kahn outlined meaningfulness, safety, and availability as the three psychological domains that ensured workers could be physically, emotionally, and cognitively engaged. Embedded within these domains were factors such as seeing value in the work being done and being valued in return; trust that the workplace encourages and honors authenticity, without fear of negative consequences, and sets clear expectations around performance; and the workplace providing both tangible and intangible resources enabling workers to perform their tasks.

Since the publication of Kahn's seminal work, the notion of engagement has been conceptualized and reconceptualized many times. Engagement was the focus of the Society for Industrial and Organizational Psychology's first journal issue in 2008 where many authors focused on whether engagement, especially employee engagement, was a new concept or simply employee satisfaction or motivation presented in a new way. What had become clear was that a single, agreed-on definition did not yet exist and that stakeholders (e.g., academics, practitioners) were "saddled with competing and inconsistent interpretations of the meaning of the construct" (Macey & Schneider, 2008, p. 3).

A few years later, Shuck's (2011) comprehensive literature review surfaced similar challenges, noting that "the lack of continuity [in approaches to employee engagement] is a significant hurdle" (p. 304) for those attempting to support organizations in strengthening employee engagement. Shuck also acknowledged that engagement "remains in a state of evolution" (p. 322) and that the "academic approach to employee engagement and the practical application and utility of the research" (p. 322) was disconnected. Much of this disconnect remains throughout the more recent work on employee and work engagement; ultimately, it may be too late to bring together the various interpretations and, perhaps, it isn't necessary.

In developing the career engagement model, we did not set out to add to the growing and disparate body of definitions, frameworks, or approaches to engagement. Rather, we found the disconnects within and between the research and our own work resulted in a need to continually fill in the blanks—in essence, "apologizing" for what appeared to be incomplete explanations of what we were observing in our practice and research. With the engagement literature, the missing piece at the time was often related to context; there seemed to be an overemphasis on individual characteristics that contributed to employee engagement or disengagement. However, we knew from the individual clients we served that most people have complex lives outside of work, often juggling many diverse roles. They were also impacted by economic challenges, technology, access to training and resources, and relationships in all arenas of their lives. It made sense to consider that all these contextual factors could easily interrupt an individual's experience of engagement at work, despite the organization's or manager's efforts to engage their workers more fully.

As our work bridged human resources/organizational development (where training and research were typically rooted in faculties of business) and counseling psychology (typically housed within faculties of education), we were also influenced by work in positive psychology; most notably Csikszentmihalyi's (1990) work on flow.

Flow Theory

In Csikszentmihalyi's (1990, 1997) early work, flow experiences (which are akin to being engaged) were presumed to be achieved by matching the level of skill to an appropriate level of challenge. If the level of challenge exceeded an individual's skill, the individual would begin to move out of flow into a state of anxiety; conversely, when challenges were too low for an individual's skills, they tended to move out of flow toward boredom.

In our own work with the flow concept (e.g., Neault, 2002), we found ourselves needing to account for more than skills, recognizing across many scenarios that *resources* could also play a critical role in one's ability to achieve and sustain flow. When equipment malfunctions, teams are understaffed, or workers do not have what they need, the ability to achieve flow depends less on individual skills than access to necessary resources. Focusing solely on skills, to some degree, blames the individual for their inability to find flow when it may be factors external to the individual, or personal characteristics other than their skills, that prevent an optimal flow experience. It is important to acknowledge that much of the more recent research on flow has reached a similar conclusion (Harmat et al., 2016).

Another problem we encountered when introducing flow to our clients was the definition that both high challenge and high skill were needed to achieve flow; conversely, the opposite of flow was apathy, which was attributed to low skill and low challenge. This implied that individuals with low skills would be excluded from flow experiences. However, in the career engagement model, we've had reports from several community support workers that their developmentally delayed clients who have very low skills have demonstrated clear signs of engagement at work when the level of challenge they are facing is appropriately low.

Career Engagement

As noted earlier, we did not initially set out to create something new, but what we had access to did not adequately explain what we were seeing with clients. Being heavily influenced from our human resource management/business backgrounds by the engagement literature, perhaps mostly by Kahn's work, and, also from our psychology backgrounds, most notably flow theory, we defined career engagement as "the current emotional and cognitive connection to one's career; it is a state in which one is focused, energized, and able to derive pleasure from activities linked to work and other life roles" (Pickerell, 2013, p. 21).

Using the word *career* was intentional and acknowledges the more recent definitions and views of career—namely that one's career comprises both paid and unpaid roles across a life span. These roles could include worker but could also include such roles as spouse/partner, child, parent, community member, leisurite, or student. Further, as originally suggested by Super back in 1957, each of these roles may become more or less salient at different times.

One's level of career engagement is realized through the dynamic interaction of challenge and capacity; capacity may be individual, organizational, or even societal. As shown in Figure 2.1, the zone of engagement is at the center, demonstrating that engagement can be achieved by anyone, from the highest performers (e.g., nuclear physicists, elite athletes) to those who may experience challenges with daily tasks (e.g., those with traumatic brain injuries or who are developmentally delayed).

Career Engagement

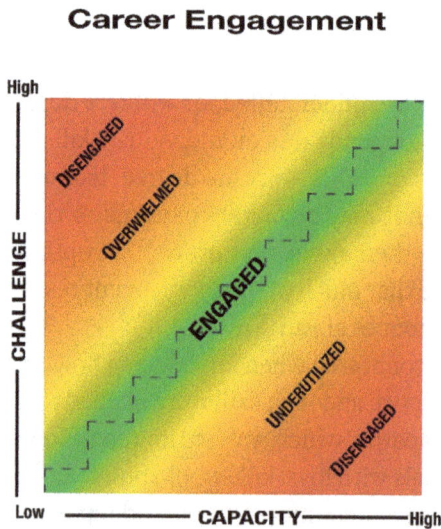

Fig. 2.1 Career engagement model.

The colors in the model are intentional, aligned to the colors in traffic lights and making the positive and negative zones immediately recognizable. Green (engaged) is a good place to be. When challenge exceeds the available capacity, individuals move out of the zone of engagement toward being overwhelmed and, without correction, become completely disengaged; this movement is visually represented in the colors, moving from green to yellow, orange (caution), and finally to red. A similar color-coded warning system is present in the other direction when challenge is too low for the available capacity. Movement in this direction results in individuals feeling underutilized, bored, and, without correction, completely disengaged.

In a 3D representation of the model, the two disengaged sections would overlap, indicating that complete disengagement feels and looks the same, regardless of the route traveled to get there (i.e., via overwhelmed or underutilized). However, the route *is* critical when considering strategies to return to the zone of engagement. An opportunity to lead an exciting new project may be a fantastic reengagement strategy for someone who became disengaged through being underutilized; the identical plan could make things considerably worse for someone who is already overwhelmed. Although flow theory (Csikszentmihalyi, 1990) also had this notion of directionality, most engagement models do not consider how someone became disengaged; they simply consider the individual's current state.

Within the zone of engagement is a dotted line, indicating that engagement is not static. In adding this aspect to the model, we were influenced by Vygotsky's (1978) zone of proximal development (ZPD), which considers the difference between the actual and potential state of development. Although the ZPD was originally conceptualized to examine real and potential problem-solving abilities in children, in the career engagement model we have used this notion of a zone of engagement to indicate the sweet spot where development can be maximized, especially with appropriate "scaffolding" (another of Vygotsky's terms). The dotted line of our model serves as a reminder that one doesn't simply achieve engagement and then stay there. Rather, there is an ongoing dynamic interaction between capacity and challenge that can shift one out of engagement toward either being overwhelmed or underutilized—and this sometimes occurs moment to moment! The notion of scaffolding serves as a good reminder that one may need to access more supports or resources, or may need less supports as a strategy to "up the challenge," in order to achieve and maintain a satisfying level of engagement.

Despite adopting a broad view of career (i.e., one that included paid and unpaid work roles across the life span), our original research focused solely on paid work as we investigated the engagement of Canadian career development professionals in an industry that was in the state of massive transformation. Combining three separate data sets, all using a work-focused quantitative survey, factor analysis revealed several factors of the two components (challenge and capacity) of the career engagement model. These are explored in the subsequent chapters but are briefly explained next.

The challenge component comprises two factors—*motivating work* and *meaningful opportunities*—which emerged in the original research (Pickerell, 2013) and have stayed relatively stable and constant following subsequent, unpublished research. In our early factor analyses, these two factors separated intrinsic challenges (which we labeled "motivating work") and extrinsic challenges (which we labeled "meaningful opportunities"). However, as we've continued to work with the model and situate it within other literature on motivation and meaning, we've recognized both intrinsic and extrinsic aspects of each of these factors. Chapters 3 and 4 explore each of these factors in more depth.

Motivating work can be described as being fascinating, stimulating, and engrossing. It occurs when motivated individuals embrace the challenges work and other life roles present.

Meaningful opportunities, on the other hand, include opportunities to grow and develop and work with interesting and talented people. Pursuing meaning and purpose contribute to career engagement.

The capacity component proved to be more complex and quite messy. The five factors that comprise this component—*resources, relationships, workload, well-being* and *fit*—emerged in more recent analyses combining several separate research projects and are slightly different from the inaugural study. The evolution of the factors, at least in part, demonstrates the complexity of the capacity component. Each is briefly outlined next, with a more thorough exploration in subsequent chapters.

Resources are both tangible and intangible; they may include skills, equipment, people, time, and/or energy. Individuals draw from available resources to respond to the challenges life presents. Depending on their roles and context, individual control over resources needed to maximize engagement may be limited.

Relationships are connections with others. In the paid work role, this will include team dynamics, relationships with coworkers, supervisors, managers, and organizational leadership. Outside of work, relationships can include family, friends, and others in the community. There is an overlap between this factor and people within the resources factor, but the separation is important. A positive relationship with one's immediate supervisor, for example, is a key driver of engagement, but the neighbor's son who mows the lawn is likely more of a resource.

Workload is used to represent the tasks or activities one must accomplish or the demands that are placed on individuals throughout their daily lives. These tasks or activities are typically associated with specific roles such as worker, parent, caregiver, or student. However, one's overall workload comprises more than the demands related to each individual role; to maximize engagement it is essential to account for the impact of the total demands across all life roles.

Well-being relates to self-care and the importance of engaging in proactive health and wellness activities such as exercising, eating well, and getting sufficient sleep. Not just concerned with physical health, well-being also considers mental health, acknowledging that factors such as stress, anxiety, and worry must be attended to.

Fit within the original research related to workplace fit, drawing on 100-plus years of literature within career development and vocational guidance, outlines that a "match" between a person's skills, interests, and characteristics is important. Within this factor, we have also included values alignment, which emphasizes the importance of personal values (e.g., helping others) in considering fit.

Applying Career Engagement

The career engagement model highlights the dynamic, ever-changing interaction between challenge and capacity. In the opening vignette of this chapter, Tom would have described himself as optimally engaged the morning before he got his layoff notice. He was perfectly suited for his work and was being recognized for his contributions. He had good relationships at work, with supervisors, managers, coworkers, and customers. His family was providing meaning and focus for his life, along with offering love and support. Financially, he had what he needed and was working toward a realistic retirement plan. Life was good.

Tom's story, however, also illustrates the precarity of sustaining optimal career engagement, even with long-term employment within a big organization. It highlights that career development is a lifelong activity and also reminds us of the interconnectedness of our many life roles. Tom left for work the morning he was laid off assuming it was just another normal day. After the meeting with his manager, plans for absolutely every part of his life felt shaken. Although he would receive a generous severance package, he worried that it wouldn't last until he found another job. When he would become eligible for employment insurance, he knew that would only cover a portion of his regular salary. The family's monthly expenses were closely aligned to his monthly income; with a new baby in the house and plans for his retirement just 5 years out, their shared family vision had not included his wife returning to work. Even his retirement plans were now out of reach. They had depended on a full pension from his employer and, instead, he would only receive a partial pension as his work was ending 5 years early. Although the company referred to this as an "early retirement opportunity," Tom was not in the financial position to retire now and worried that even if he found another job, it wouldn't pay as much and he wouldn't accrue enough pension benefits to achieve his 5-year plans.

Activities

2.1   Level of Engagement

Now that you have learned about career engagement, take a moment to assess where you would plot yourself on the model overall. Think big picture, without feeling overly constrained by any specific role.

If generally engaged, consider which direction you tend to go when feeling less engaged. Do you move toward feeling overwhelmed or underutilized?

As the experience of career engagement can be impacted by your various roles, reflect on which roles contribute to you being in the zone of engagement and which move you toward being overwhelmed and/or underutilized.

Here's an example for Tom. He's indicated being quite overwhelmed right now, in all areas of his life. He feels blindsided by being laid off and acknowledges that he may still be in shock. He worries that if he stays off work too long, he may slip into feeling underutilized and perhaps completely disengaged. However, when he considers his financial situation, he can't imagine moving out of overwhelmed any time soon.

Career Engagement

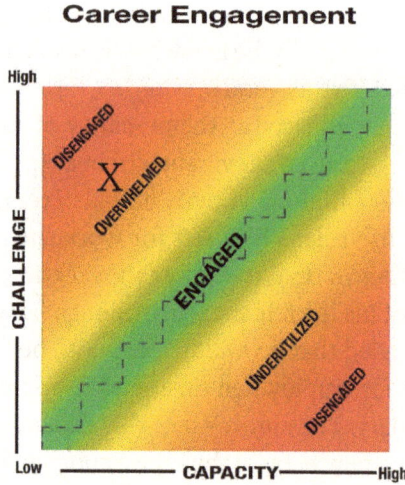

IMG. 2.2

Now it's your turn. Where would you plot yourself on the model overall? Thinking of your key roles individually, would you plot yourself in a different zone of the model? If so, please indicate them as well.

Career Engagement

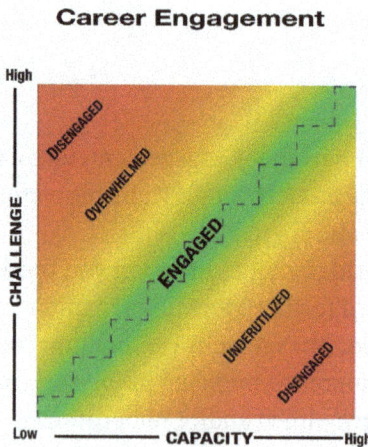

IMG. 2.3

Five Big Ideas

1. **Career engagement is not static.** It is ever-changing and realized through the dynamic interaction of challenge and capacity. As one of those components shifts, your experience of career engagement will too. As such, it is important to continuously monitor your engagement, catching early movement away from engagement toward feeling overwhelmed or underutilized and making small shifts to reestablish the balance.

2. **Career engagement is both holistic and specific.** Individuals can have an over-all sense of being engaged, overwhelmed, or underutilized, but when focusing in on a specific role, things can change quite drastically. Remain aware of which roles are more likely to keep you engaged and which are more likely to have you feeling overwhelmed or underutilized.

3. **Disengaged is disengaged.** The experience of being actively disengaged is the same regardless of the route—being overwhelmed or underutilized. Effective strategies for returning to the zone of engagement, however, will be completely dependent on the route taken to become disengaged. An exciting new opportunity may promote reengagement for those feeling bored and underutilized but could be highly problematic for those who are already overwhelmed and experiencing stress-related burnout.

4. **A dual experience is possible.** With most people juggling multiple roles concur-rently, it is possible to be overwhelmed within one role and underutilized within another. Interestingly, these concurrent experiences can cancel each other out (i.e., a balance of being overwhelmed in one role and underutilized in another may leave someone feeling generally okay). However, concurrent extremes of being overwhelmed and underutilized can also be exhausting and frustrating as one makes big shifts from one role's responsibilities to the other's.

5. **Career engagement comprises challenge and capacity.** These two compo-nents dynamically interact and must be relatively evenly balanced for optimal career engagement to be achieved. Each of these components are influenced by a set of factors. For challenge, the factors are motivating work and meaningful opportunities; for capacity, the factors are resources, relationships, workload, well-being, and fit.

References

Csikszentmihalyi, M. (1990). *Flow: The psychology of optimal experience*. Harper & Row.

Csikszentmihalyi, M. (1997). *Finding flow*. HarperCollins.

Harmat, L., Andersen, F. Ø, Ullén, F., Wright, J. et Sadlo, G. (dir.) (2016). *Flow experience: Empirical research and applications*. Springer.

Kahn, W. A. (1990). Psychological conditions of personal engagement and disengagement at work. *The Academy of Management Journal, 33*(4), 692–724. https://www.talenteck.com/academic/Kahn-1990.pdf

Macey, W. H., & Schneider, B. (2008). The meaning of employee engagement. *Industrial and Organizational Psychology, 1*(1), 3–30. http://dx.doi.org/10.1111%2Fj.1754-9434.2007.0002.x

Neault, R. (2002). Thriving in the new millennium: Career management in the changing world of work. *Canadian Journal of Career Development, 1*(1), 11–21. https://cjcd-rcdc.ceric.ca/index.php/cjcd/article/view/66/89

Pickerell, D. (2013). *Examining the career engagement of Canadian career development practitioners* [Unpublished doctoral dissertation]. Fielding Graduate University.

Shuck, B. (2011). Four emerging perspectives of employee engagement: An integrative literature review. *Human Resource Development Review, 10*(3), 304–328. https://doi.org/10.1177/1534484311410840

Super, D. E. (1957). *The psychology of careers.* Harper & Row.

Vygotsky, L. S. (1978). *Mind and society: The development of higher psychological processes* (M. Cole, V. John-Steiner, S. Scribner, & E. Souberman, Eds.). Harvard University Press. https://doi.org/10.2307/j.ctvjf9vz4

Figure Credits

CHAPTER THREE

Challenge: Motivating Work

IMG. 3.1

Arthur, now 78, has no intention of ever retiring. He has been working continuously for the past 65 years after leaving school when he was only 13. Although starting out as a general laborer, he has acquired a lot of skills in 65 years of working and loves to keep learning.

Twenty years ago, the organization where Arthur worked was going through the early stages of a merger. It quickly became clear that postsecondary education and specific certifications would be considered essential job requirements in the new corporate structure. Arthur, and a small group of coworkers who had similarly worked their way up through the ranks, pooled their savings, consulted with lawyers and bankers, and put together a counteroffer. Arthur and his colleagues now own the company!

Over the years, Arthur's day-to-day work has varied considerably: He knows that's part of what's kept him so interested. He loves problem solving and has developed an unusual ability to see challenges as intriguing and stimulating. Especially since becoming a part owner of the company, Arthur knows that his work is making a significant difference. He is proud that he's played a key role in creating employment opportunities for people like him who, although they may have limited formal education, have a great attitude, are committed to continuous learning, and have all the skills needed to get the job done.

Exploring the Factor: Motivating Work

In the factor analysis of our preliminary career engagement research (Pickerell, 2013), the challenge component revealed two factors: *motivating work* and *meaningful opportunities*. Although questions from the pilot survey seemed to cluster into motivation as intrinsic (e.g., "My work is fascinating to me") and meaning as more extrinsic (e.g., "I don't think my employer is making the best use of my talents" [which was reverse scored]), we have since expanded both aspects of challenge to recognize intrinsic and extrinsic influences.

Although much has been written about motivation, crossing cultures and continents over thousands of years of recorded history, McInerny (2019), in his editorial for a special issue on motivation for *Educational Psychology*, acknowledged that over the past 100-plus years the research has been dominated by Western influences and has not fully resonated with diverse cultural groups. More recently, research has once again crossed cultures and contexts, recognizing that motivation is impacted by intrinsic and extrinsic influences, personal style, and even perceptions of social justice and equity.

In one recent example of cross-cultural research on motivation, Shkoler and Kimura (2020) investigated the effects of intrinsic and extrinsic motivation on job engagement in both Israel and Japan. These researchers not only found country differences in their results but also differences across employee status (i.e., working students versus nonstudent employees). Their findings have implications for employee motivation and engagement in a context of global mobility, increasing cultural diversity in the workplace, and an expanding gap between secure and precarious employment. They also apply to Arthur's situation in our opening vignette—although one might deem buying the company as a risky, precarious adventure when compared to staying on as a salaried employee, Arthur found a renewed motivation in changing his employment status.

Both academic and self-help literature offer an abundance of material on the differences between intrinsic and extrinsic motivation. For example, in a recent Healthline article, Santos-Longhurst (2019) provided several examples of both types of motivators. Intrinsic motivation does not require external rewards; rather, individuals engage in activities because they enjoy them, find them challenging and/or interesting, or are aiming to meet biological or psychological needs. Intrinsic motivators may include curiosity, fascination, fun, autonomy, competence, satisfaction, or relaxation. Extrinsic motivation, on the other hand, may be driven by striving for a reward or recognition, avoiding punishment or other negative consequences, or because an activity is required.

Differences in intrinsic and extrinsic motivation may be slight—and may vary between individuals. One individual might read a particular book because it has been assigned by a teacher and there will be a quiz on the contents (extrinsic motivation comes from the teacher requiring the activity and evaluating the outcome; motivation to engage with the book will be even higher if the individual has a strong desire to avoid low marks). Another individual might read the same book because the topic is fascinating, reading is relaxing, and other books by the same author have been enjoyable (intrinsic motivation).

In recent years, gamification has offered a new approach to motivation in settings as diverse as schools, workplaces, and online gaming communities. Gamification has elements of both intrinsic and extrinsic motivation and has also been linked to engagement (Simon Fraser University, 2018). Turning an activity into a game can be either formal (i.e., intentionally creating a game for the use of others) or informal (i.e., converting an everyday, perhaps uninspiring, activity into a game through competition, collaboration, creative problem solving, or external rewards such as badges or gift certificates). Within our own team at Life Strategies Ltd., for example, we've occasionally used a "ticky contest" to inspire our team members to work through tasks that have become either overwhelming or boring and a bit of a slog. The rules are simple. Each person places a Post-It note beside their computer and uses a tally mark (ticky) to indicate each completed task, regardless of how much time the task takes (i.e., a 30-second task earns the same ticky point as a 30-minute task). At the end of a specified period (generally a couple of days), each person earns a gift card according to the number of tasks they've completed; the overall winner gets the largest gift card value, but everyone wins something. Not surprisingly, team members work to get the "quick wins" finished first. In the span of just a few hours, we've sometimes crossed well over a hundred tasks off our combined lists! Although this could seem like busywork or facilitating distraction from the "real" work that needs doing, it's incredibly invigorating. Team members become noticeably reenergized and engaged and interested in their work once the clutter of small tasks that have been weighing them down has been removed. After the first few hours, they are left with the bigger tasks that require more focused attention—and they now have the clear head space to get them done.

In our career engagement model, Ford and Smith's (2020) book, *Motivating Self and Others*, would sit at the intersection of *motivating work* and *meaningful opportunities*. Similar to Csikszentmihalyi's (1990) foundational work on flow, Ford and Smith discussed the motivating impact of "goal–life alignment and 'thriving with social purpose' [to] inspire optimal functioning and enhance life meaning" (p. i). Taking a systems perspective, they acknowledged that motivation doesn't exist in a vacuum or solely within the individual. Rather, motivation is enriched by meaning—the two factors that, combined, comprise *challenge* in career engagement. Also, they acknowledged that *work* motivation can't be fully separated from motivation in other life roles, recognizing the importance of aligning one's goals across all life arenas in order to maximize and sustain optimal engagement.

Applying Career Engagement

In the opening vignette for this chapter, Arthur had momentarily lost motivation for his work. As the anticipated merger approached, he realized that without further education or credentials he wouldn't be permitted to keep doing the work that fascinated and stimulated him. The only work in the new organization that he'd be qualified for sounded boring and unimportant; he saw it as work that anyone could do, not work that would capitalize on his years of experience within the company.

As he considered his options, however, Arthur also began to feel overwhelmed. At 58 years of age, he was concerned about having to go back to school in order to keep his job if the merger proceeded. He was frightened by the possibility that he might need to find a new employer. Although his finances were in good shape and he could afford to retire, he wasn't ready to—he thrived at work and loved the structure, social connections, and purpose that it offered to his life.

Although Arthur loved to learn, he couldn't imagine taking high school courses that didn't seem relevant to his current work. When he considered the possibility of taking some of the certification courses that would become required, he pictured himself dying of boredom. Not only had he been doing the work for 45 years at the time, he was one of the organization's most popular trainers. Everyone who knew him agreed; it would be crazy to send him back to school to get certified in work that he was successfully training others to do.

However, the idea of actually buying the company was exciting and challenging. He loved the strategic conversations with his colleagues about how to stall the merger and put their own offer forward. The long days (and nights) flew by as they put a plan together and arranged the financing. There were certainly overwhelming moments as well, but those days were far from boring! The moment the group realized that the counteroffer was a realistic possibility, they became laser focused on writing the winning bid.

Arthur has never regretted his decision to join the team that bought the company. Twenty years later, he still finds the work fascinating and appreciates that each day brings new challenges. Friends and family members often comment on how active his mind is—it never seems to stop! Most important to Arthur, though, is that he knows his work matters. He is continuing to make a vital contribution to his industry, his employees, and his community. His work is both motivating and meaningful. The next chapter will expand more on meaningful opportunities as the second factor within the challenge component.

Activities

3.1   Unpacking Motivation

Reflect on a time that you felt highly motivated by a task or activity. Contrast that with a time that seemed to drag by, and you just couldn't dredge up the motivation to get the task off your plate. What, specifically, contributed to those two very different experiences?

We'll start with an example from Arthur. He chose to look back to the time of the merger.

When I was motivated ...	When I couldn't get motivated ...
Putting together the offer to purchase the company	Imagining myself in the company if the merger went through
What was motivating me?	**What was demotivating me?**
A sense of contributing to something big	Frustration that the new requirements for education and credentials would exclude me from work I'd been doing successfully for years
Helping people I cared about	Fear of trying to find a new employer
Working toward a specific, time-sensitive goal	Embarrassed by my limited education and that coworkers and supervisors would find out
A chance to be creative and to solve problems	The work I'd be demoted to felt meaningless
Knowing that there was a very good chance of succeeding in buying the company	I felt disrespected and hopeless

Now it's your turn.

When I was motivated ...	When I couldn't get motivated ...
What was motivating me?	**What was demotivating me?**

What was motivating me?	What was demotivating me?
....	....
....	....
....	....
....	....
....	....
....	....
....	....
....	....
....	....
....	....
....	....
....	....
....	....
....	....
....	....
....	....
....	....
....	....
....	....
....	....

3.2   Intrinsic versus Extrinsic Motivation

We can't simply push a button or turn a switch to motivate ourselves or others—although many parents, teachers, supervisors, and spouses wish that button or switch existed! However, there are tangible actions and attitudes that can contribute to creating a motivating environment.

The table that follows lists some typical intrinsic and extrinsic motivators. Think of an upcoming project that you may need some extra motivation to complete. Reflect on the motivators on the list; there's space to add more if you think of something that would better serve as a motivator for you. Use the columns provided to indicate specific actions that you or others can take to ignite at least six of the motivators to inspire you to complete your upcoming project.

Here's an example from Arthur:

My upcoming project:

We're almost ready to launch a new system for managing payroll and benefits. I'm not a computer geek, and I know there's going to be resistance from many employees. I know it's important but it's hard to get motivated to develop the necessary training modules.

Intrinsic motivators	What I can do	Extrinsic motivators	What others can/will do
Fun	Make the training interesting; build in gamification/prizes.	Money	There's an incentive from the supplier for launching on time.
Believe in the cause	This is the right system. I believe in it.	Praise and recognition	
Happiness		Grades	
Health		Career building	
Connect to others		Avoid punishment	We'll have duplicate costs if we can't switch systems on time.
Creativity	I love working from a blank slate when building training.	Please others	The accounting and HR teams have worked *so* hard for this.
Intellectual stimulation	This is intriguing. I have to learn enough to teach it.	Keep up appearances	I said I'd build the training—and my training is usually popular.
Relaxation		Follow orders	

Now it's your turn.

My upcoming project:

....

....

Intrinsic motivators	What I can do	Extrinsic motivators	What others can do
Fun	....	Money	....
	....		....
	....		....
	....		....
Believe in the cause	....	Praise and recognition	....
	....		....
	....		....
	....		....
Happiness	....	Grades	....
	....		....
	....		....
	....		....
Health	....	Career building	....
	....		....
	....		....
	....		....

Intrinsic motivators	What I can do	Extrinsic motivators	What others can do
Connect to others	....	Avoid punishment	....
	....		....
	....		....
	....		....
	....		....
Creativity	....	Please others	....
	....		....
	....		....
	....		....
	....		....
Intellectual stimulation	....	Keep up appearances	....
	....		....
	....		....
	....		....
	....		....
Relaxation	....	Follow orders	....
	....		....
	....		....
	....		....
	....		....

Intrinsic motivators	What I can do	Extrinsic motivators	What others can do
....	....	....	....
....	....	....	....
....	....	....	....
....	....	....	....
....	....	....	....
....	....	....	....
....	....	....	....
....	....	....	....
....	....	....	....
....	....	....	....
....	....	....	....
....	....	....	....
....	....	....	....
....	....	....	....
....	....	....	....

Five Big Ideas

1. **Gamify to motivate.** You can turn almost any activity into a game—either just for yourself or in competition or collaboration with others. Motivating games have rules, goals, and rewards. You know where you're heading, and it's worth the effort to get there. Games are intriguing, inspiring, and fun!

2. **You can outgrow motivation.** At some point things that used to be fascinating and stimulating no longer hold your attention in the same way; instead they become routine and boring. Monitor your motivation and, when you find yourself shifting away from the zone of optimal engagement into boredom, make minor

or major adjustments to increase the challenges you are facing or to make your activities more fun and inspiring.

3. **You can reach your capacity limit.** Taking on an ever-increasing level of challenge isn't sustainable. Engagement is inextricably linked to a *balance* between challenge and capacity—even the most motivating activity will leave you exhausted and disengaged if your capacity/resources are stretched beyond your ability to pull it off. Capacity needs replenishing, and sometimes the most motivating activity is simply to relax and have fun.

4. **Motivation is both intrinsic and extrinsic.** Sometimes you just need to dredge up motivation within yourself to get a task accomplished. Consider gamification or simply bringing some fun into it. Other times, focusing on external forces can be motivating. Working on a team, avoiding penalties, the possibility of earning a bonus or winning an award, or recognition from someone important to you can all contribute to motivating you to accomplish a task.

5. **Reignite your passion.** Sometimes it's hard to find motivation within yourself, and external motivators are no longer inspiring. Take time to reflect on what you're doing—and why. Key to motivation is believing in the cause and having a clear goal. Make small adjustments before becoming fully disengaged. Search for opportunities to be creative, to connect with others on shared goals, or simply to have some fun!

References

Csikszentmihalyi, M. (1990). *Flow: The psychology of optimal experience.* Harper & Row.

Ford, M. E., Smith, P. R., & Cambridge Core EBA eBooks Complete Collection. (2020). *Motivating self and others: Thriving with social purpose, life meaning, and the pursuit of core personal goals.* Cambridge University Press.

McInerney, D. M. (2019). Motivation. *Educational Psychology (Dorchester-on-Thames), 39*(4), 427–429. https://doi.org/10.1080/01443410.2019.1600774

Pickerell, D. (2013). *Examining the career engagement of Canadian career development practitioners* [Unpublished doctoral dissertation]. Fielding Graduate University.

Santos-Longhurst (2019, February 11). *Intrinsic motivation: How to pick up healthy motivation techniques.* Healthline. https://www.healthline.com/health/intrinsic-motivation

Shkoler, O., & Kimura, T. (2020). How does work motivation impact employees' investment at work and their job engagement? A moderated-moderation perspective through an international lens. *Frontiers in Psychology, 11*(38). https://doi.org/10.3389/fpsyg.2020.00038

Simon Fraser University. (2018). *Gamification, motivation, and engagement.* https://wiki.its.sfu.ca/permanent/learning/index.php/Gamification,_Motivation_and_Engagement

Figure Credit

CHAPTER FOUR

Challenge: Meaningful Opportunities

IMG. 4.1

Hui-ying, although born in Canada, had been raised by parents who had emigrated from China just the year before she was born. Her mother was a professor at a prestigious university where, Hui-ying, now 18, could attend almost for free due to a tuition-waiver program for dependents of faculty members. Both of Hui-ying's parents highly valued formal education—even the name they had chosen for their baby girl reflected that; translated to English, Hui-ying means "intelligent" or "smart." Although she consistently got good grades in school, it hadn't come easy for Hui-ying. Her parents had invested in tutors, online courses, summer school, and endless hours of homework support to ensure that she would have the grades to get accepted into her mother's university as it was rated amongst the top in the world!

However, Hui-ying didn't want to go to university—at least not right now. What she really loved to do was work with her hands. She had taken a couple of woodworking electives at school and discovered a love for making fine furniture, especially with intricate carvings and hand-turned spindles. Her teachers commented on her giftedness as a carpenter and encouraged her to consider applying to some woodworking programs after graduation, preparing her to pursue an apprenticeship.

Exploring the Factor: Meaningful Opportunities

Challenge is one of the two main components of the career engagement model; *meaningful opportunities* is one of the two factors that challenge comprises. To achieve and sustain an optimal level of engagement, at work, school, or in other life roles, there needs to be an appropriate balance between challenge and capacity. As previously mentioned, too much challenge is overwhelming; too little, on the other hand, leaves one feeling underutilized and enroute to becoming disengaged.

Hui-ying, in our vignette, struggles in terms of the capacity to achieve the academic success that her parents are looking for. Her willingness to continue to pursue her parents' academic dream is waning, in part because she doesn't anticipate finding anything personally meaningful to her at her mother's university. Instead, Hui-ying found meaningful opportunities within woodworking—similar to Csikszentmihalyi's (1990) description of a *flow* experience, when working on an intricate woodworking project, Hui-ying found herself focused, fully engaged, and losing track of time.

Meaningful opportunities *are* engaging, as confirmed by Allan et al. (2019) in a metanalysis comprising 44 articles. They found large correlations between meaningful work and work engagement, commitment, and job satisfaction and moderate to large correlations with life satisfaction, life meaning, general health, and withdrawal intentions; in essence, meaningful work matters. In Hui-ying's case, the lack of meaning in her academic studies, combined with how hard she was finding her current course load, was wearing her down. She was losing interest in continuing to university, and her mental and physical health was beginning to suffer. This fit with Allan et al.'s findings that lack of meaning had impacts beyond one's work role, influencing meaning and satisfaction in other life arenas along with one's general health and well-being.

When Hui-ying couldn't see the point of going to university (i.e., it didn't seem meaningful to her), she began to look toward her future with dread rather than hope. Although generally an optimistic person, she couldn't visualize the possibility of success at university. However, optimism is important; it has been shown to be the single best predictor of both career success and job satisfaction (Neault, 2002). Finding meaning in the work you're doing fuels hope and optimism and spills over into all your interconnected life roles. For Hui-ying to reengage with school and to prepare for a career in which she could thrive, it would be important to find meaningful opportunities.

Bailey et al. (2019), in their introduction to a special issue of the *Journal of Management Studies* on the topic of meaningful work, acknowledged that "meaningfulness is a multi-level construct" (p. 482). It is one of relatively few constructs that has bridged academic silos, with research and publications in "management studies, psychology, social psychology, human resource management/development, political theory, theology, philosophy, ethics, and sociology" (p. 482). Despite, or perhaps because of this breadth of interest, there is little consensus at this point about a definition for meaningfulness. In general, though, there's an understanding that meaningful work finds a balance between being and doing, and self versus others (Lips-Wiersma & Wright, 2012). Similar to our focus on context in the career engagement model, Bailey et al. noted an emerging recognition, supported by social constructivist approaches, that meaningful work is not simply the subjective experience of an individual (i.e., housed solely within oneself) but, rather, is impacted by dynamic organizational, economic, and political structures. Despite their best attempts, organizations can't *make* work meaningful for an individual, nor can an individual be held solely responsible for not finding meaning in work that makes no sense. They also acknowledge the episodic nature of meaningful work—just as within the career engagement model, one doesn't achieve engagement and then stay there; any work (paid or unpaid) is unlikely to be experienced as meaningful all day, every day. Rather, one can hope to find meaning overall, or most of the time, in the tasks that need to be accomplished each day.

This has implications for Hui-ying's situation. Her parents, as much as they've tried to support her academic success, can't make university meaningful for her. However, Hui-ying also can't simply work harder to change her attitude; instead, she needs to find some meaningful opportunities that challenge and engage her, opportunities that fit with her abilities and personal characteristics.

Martela and Pessi (2018) identified three dimensions of meaningful work: *work significance*, *broader purpose*, and *self-realization*. Within the career engagement model, meaningful work is work that you know is serving a great purpose; it's work that matters, makes a difference, and that you are contributing to in a unique and important way.

"Job crafting" (i.e., employees redesigning their work to create a better fit) has also been linked to the ideas of meaningful work and engagement (Vermooten et al., 2019). This notion of "job crafting" might need to be modified for Hui-ying as she considers postsecondary options. According to Vermooten and colleagues, there's no need to sit passively as you watch yourself become disengaged from work that has lost meaning. Instead, consider what changes (whether micro or more significant) might help to rediscover meaning. Not all changes can be made in isolation. Job crafting in the workplace, for example, may require the collaboration of a supervisor or manager; within a postsecondary context, "program crafting" may involve creative interdisciplinary negotiations or taking electives from other faculties or institutions.

Viktor Frankl is known for his writing about "man's search for meaning in work and activities for positive change" (von Devivere, 2018, p. 9). Similar to Bailey et al. (2019), von Devivere identified the pervasive, interdisciplinary interest in a universal quest for meaning and purpose. Meaning matters.

Applying Career Engagement

As mentioned, within the career engagement model, one of the components contributing to challenge is "meaningful opportunities." Although Hui-ying understood the value her parents placed on a prestigious university education, followed by an equally prestigious professional career, she just couldn't see herself successfully completing a degree that she personally found meaningless. At her parents' strong request, Hui-ying did apply to her mother's university—and her application was accepted. However, once there she struggled even more than she had in high school. Class sizes were much larger, leaving little access to hands-on support or practical demonstrations of complex concepts. At the end of the first term, Hui-ying's marks were very poor; by the end of the second term, she was placed on academic probation.

Although her parents continued to invest in tutors, it became clear that Hui-ying was not going to succeed at university; her mental health deteriorated, and she became anxious about attending university, completing assignments, and maintaining social connections. Hui-ying became more and more withdrawn. Her only joy was making small jewelry boxes in the woodworking shop she had set up in her parents' garage. By the end of her 2nd year, Hui-ying had failed enough courses that she was required to withdraw from the university for 12 months. Although she was ashamed by this, and was upset to have disappointed her parents, especially after all they had invested to ensure she would successfully complete university, Hui-ying also experienced an immediate sense of relief.

Hui-ying and her parents agreed that it would be important for her to not just sit at home for her 12 months away from the university. However, it seemed clear from all their efforts over the past 2 years that more tutoring and taking similar courses at a community college were unlikely to improve Hui-ying's grades or mental health. Really committed to pursuing training in woodworking, Hui-ying discovered a pre-apprenticeship program in fine woodworking, and her parents agreed to support her for one term to see how she did.

Hui-ying surprised even herself. Once she was enrolled in courses that seemed "meaningful" to her, she was able to keep up with the readings and was successful even in the most academic courses and assignments. She went from failing grades to consistently earning As and Bs.

Hui-ying's parents were pleased to see her happy again, successful at school, and regaining her confidence. However, they still highly valued university education; that was deeply ingrained in their cultural heritage. Recognizing that Hui-ying would need work that interested her to thrive, they agreed to explore university options together that would allow Hui-ying to pursue her interest and talent in woodworking while attaining a prestigious degree and career; this fits with Vermooten et al.'s (2019) discussion of "job-crafting" to create meaningful opportunities. Hui-ying contacted a career counselor who helped her identify university programs in conservation and restoration; the more she learned about the meticulous woodworking projects in museums and heritage buildings, the more excited she got. Hui-ying identified a relevant undergraduate program at her mother's university and set her sights on qualifying for a graduate program in a prestigious university in Europe.

Hui-ying's academic studies had taken on a very different meaning to her. Although the work was challenging, it was fully engaging. She understood what she was studying and how it fit with her future career goals—and she also understood that maintaining a high GPA was essential if she wanted to move on to a competitive master's degree. With meaning, purpose, reduced anxiety about the future, and less tension with her parents, Hui-ying was well positioned to succeed. She maintained her A grades and put her learning to immediate use by volunteering on furniture restoration projects for the museum at her university.

Interestingly, another meaning to the name Hui-ying's parents had given her was "clever." She could identify with that much more than simply intelligent or smart, which had been the meanings her parents had emphasized throughout her childhood and high school years. Now that she'd found meaning in her work, she was able to demonstrate her cleverness through her designs, creative use of resources, and research into how to restore historical artifacts and buildings using materials available today.

Activities

4.1 Meaningful Opportunities

Reflect on a challenging activity that felt particularly engaging for you (i.e., you felt well suited for it and it felt meaningful to participate in). Briefly describe the activity and identify the specific elements that made it particularly meaningful.

Here's an example from Hui-ying.

> I really enjoyed a volunteer project restoring an antique armoire that had been used in the home of the first prime minister of Canada. It was exciting to use some of the special techniques that I learned in the fine woodworking program. However, it was so much better because I now have the academic training to research the historical period, learn more about the type of wood and hardware used, and carefully document the restoration work that I did to ensure a detailed historical record for this priceless piece of furniture.

Now it's your turn.

4.2 Know Your Why!

There are many compelling YouTube videos featuring comedian and motivational speaker, Michael Jr. (Habeeb, 2015) on the theme of "know your why." He emphasizes (and vividly illustrates) the difference in performance that come from knowing *why* you are doing something. This understanding of purpose can make a huge difference in your ability to achieve and maintain career engagement. Beyond having a plan for *what* to do, it's important to take time to reflect on *why* those activities will matter. Use this activity to reflect on your *why* for your anticipated next step in your career or another significant life role.

Hui-ying knew *what* her parents expected her to do and, as a respectful daughter, she really wanted to meet their high expectations for her and to make them proud. However, without knowing her *why*, she kept slipping further and further away from success. Here's a start to her "Know Your Why!" activity.

What? Complete program at Mom's university that leads to a prestigious job.

Why? To prepare for a career in restoration and conservation and to qualify for a competitive graduate degree to complete my studies, I'll need to keep my GPA at A or above to get into the master's program that I want.

As Hui-ying found her why for academic studies, her marks seemed to miraculously improve, despite previous very serious challenges with her academic performance. Now it's your turn. Identify something that you're currently working on and, more importantly, why that activity is meaningful to you.

What?

....

....

....

....

Why?

....

....

....

....

4.3 Finding Your 5Ps: Pride, Passion, Purpose, Performance, and Poise

Our colleague, Dr. Kris Magnusson (Neault, 2012), has developed a comprehensive framework for helping individuals identify their strengths and to find meaning and purpose in their work. First, identify an accomplishment—something you take particular *pride* in. Next, reflect on what contributed to that accomplishment; your unique combination of skills, attitudes, values, beliefs, and interests can help to point to your *passion*. Look for meaningful opportunities to do more of what you love—fulfilling your *purpose*. As you live out your purpose through pursuing meaningful opportunities (i.e., performance), you'll generally find that you get better at what you're doing and more confident in doing it. *Poise* is the natural result!

Hui-ying reflected on her turnaround at school. For her 5P activity, she focused once again on her volunteer project for the museum, restoring the first prime minister's armoire.

Pride: The finished armoire is beautiful; there is no indication at all that there had been previous damage or that it had been recently restored. Everyone at the museum was impressed and thrilled that it turned out so well. It had been in storage for a long time!

Passion: I love detailed and delicate woodworking and have learned that I particularly enjoy working on historically important projects where research is important to ensure that I get it just right!

Purpose: I know deep in my heart that I'm on the right track for my career now. I can't imagine ever getting tired of working with wood in restoration and conservation of historic buildings and artifacts!

Performance: Through school projects and volunteer work, I'm getting amazing experiences and getting to work with experts in conservation and restoration. The days just fly by.

Poise: I still have so much to learn, so I wouldn't say that I've achieved poise yet—but it's coming. It's especially exciting (and builds my confidence) to have museum experts comment on the great work that I'm doing for them. I love what I'm doing!

Now it's your turn. Use the space provided to identify your own 5P's. Begin by identifying something that you already do quite well and are proud of, then walk through the rest of the activity to reflect on how persistently pursuing meaningful opportunities can result in confidence and career engagement.

Pride:

....

....

Passion:

....

....

Purpose:

....

....

Performance:

....

....

Poise:

....

....

Adapted from Roberta Neault, *Career Strategies for a Lifetime of Success*. Copyright © 2012 by Life Strategies Ltd. Reprinted with permission.

Five Big Ideas

1. **Meaning is individually and, to some extent, culturally defined.** What one person or group finds meaningful, others may not. In looking for, and even communicating about, meaningful opportunities, it's important not to make assumptions but, rather, to fully unpack what it is about specific types of opportunities that make them meaningful to you.
2. **Meaningful opportunities are all around you.** Optimal career engagement involves the dynamic interaction of activities across all your life roles. There may

be times when work seems less meaningful. To reignite engagement, consider looking for meaningful opportunities at home, through professional development, or by volunteering on a community project.

3. **Know your why.** Comedian Michael Jr. (Habeeb, 2015) vividly illustrates how knowing your purpose for an activity (i.e., *why* you're doing it) dramatically impacts performance. Meaning matters. Look for meaning and purpose in all you do.

4. **Don't settle.** Sometimes our work tasks, courses in school, or other required activities are not intrinsically meaningful. However, without finding meaning and purpose it can be hard to stay on task. Get creative—engage in "job crafting" or "design thinking" to make the big or little shifts that will help you find meaning in accomplishing everyday activities.

5. **Know your limits.** Pursuing meaningful opportunities, although highly engaging and even somewhat addictive, can become exhausting. Meaningful opportunities comprise just one factor contributing to challenge in the career engagement model. However, pursuing them beyond your capacity can be overwhelming and, ultimately, disengaging. Aligning challenge and capacity is key.

References

Allan, B. A., Batz-Barbarich, C., Sterling, H. M., & Tay, L. (2019). Outcomes of meaningful work: A meta analysis. *Journal of Management Studies, 56*(3), 500–528. https://doi.org/10.1111/joms.12406

Bailey, C., Lips-Wiersma, M., Madden, A., Yeoman, R., Thompson, M., & Chalofsky, N. (2019). The five paradoxes of meaningful work: Introduction to the special issue "Meaningful work: Prospects for the 21st century." *Journal of Management Studies, 56*(3), 481–499. https://doi.org/10.1111/joms.12422

Csikszentmihalyi, M. (1990). *Flow: The psychology of optimal experience.* Harper & Row.

Habeeb, S. (2015, September 10). *Michael Jr: Know your why* [Video]. YouTube. https://www.youtube.com/watch?v=LZe5y2D6oYU

Lips-Wiersma, M., & Wright, S. (2012). Measuring the meaning of meaningful work: Development and validation of the Comprehensive Meaningful Work Scale (CMWS). *Group and Organization Management, 37*, 665–685. https://doi.org/10.1177%2F1059601112461578

Martela, F., & Pessi, A. B. (2018). Significant work is about self-realization and broader purpose: Defining the key dimensions of meaningful work. *Frontiers in Psychology, 9*(363). https://dx.doi.org/10.3389%2Ffpsyg.2018.00363

Neault, R. A. (2002). Thriving in the new millennium: Career management in the changing world of work. *Canadian Journal of Career Development, 1*(1), 11–21. https://cjcd.scholasticahq.com/article/14098.pdf

Neault, R. (2012). *Career strategies for a lifetime of success* (3rd ed.). Life Strategies.

Vermooten, N., Boonzaier, B., & Kidd, M. (2019). Job crafting, proactive personality and meaningful work: Implications for employee engagement and turnover intention. *SA Journal of Industrial Psychology, 45*, a1567. https://doi.org/10.4102/sajip.v45i0.1567

von Devivere, B. (2018). *Meaningful work: Viktor Frankl's legacy for the 21st century.* Springer.

Figure Credit

IMG 4.1: Copyright © 2021 Depositphotos/Iren_Miller.

CHAPTER FIVE

Capacity: Resources

OPENING VIGNETTE

IMG. 5.1

Esme and Elosie just celebrated their 15th anniversary, having been inseparable after meeting at college orientation almost 20 years ago. Elosie is a conservation officer with a degree in fish and wildlife management; her area of specialty and focus is stream and river conservation. She has recently taken on a special project leading a team, alongside a biologist, that will focus on dealing with invasive plant species in local waterways. Esme is a teacher in the local middle school, teaching mostly Grade 6/7 split classes. She coaches the basketball and tennis teams, was Teacher of the Year last year, and tutors students from the local high school two evenings a week.

Esme and Elosie bought their first home about a year ago, an older but well-maintained split level with a garage that has been partially converted to a suite that brings in some rental income to help with the mortgage. They live in a small semi-rural community, about 90 minutes from their region's major urban center and international airport and about 25 minutes from a national forest. They are estranged from Esme's parents and have been since Esme first let them know that she and Elosie were living together as a couple, not long after leaving home for college. They do see Esme's older sister from time to time, but visits are limited. Elosie's family has more than made up for the lack of connections with Esme's family. Although an only child, Elosie has her parents, aunts and uncles, and many cousins that she is quite close to, getting together as often as they can though living hundreds of miles apart.

Up until quite recently Esme and Elosie would have said life was as perfect as it could be. However, Elosie had a nasty fall near a local stream, resulting in a broken wrist, a few badly bruised ribs, and a mild concussion. Although her injuries were not overly serious, and could have been much worse, she will be off work for several weeks. In addition, another huge round of budget cuts has hit Esme's school, forcing her to continue to be even more creative in lesson planning and to subsidize lessons/activities from her own resources.

Exploring the Factor: Resources

Capacity is one of the two components, along with *challenge*, that comprise the career engagement model. *Resources* is the first factor that emerged within capacity and connects back to Neault's (2006) extension of Csikszentmihalyi's (1990) notion of flow, which, at that time, focused solely on an individual's *skill* to effectively deal with challenges. Our experience with the long-term unemployed in the 90s and with individuals in corporate settings who were constantly being expected to reach stretch targets and to do more with less led to us always referring to skills/*resources* when introducing the flow model to our clients. Within career engagement, the resources factor comprises both individual attributes, such as skills, along with external/contextual resources such as equipment, supplies, time, and even people.

Esme and Elosie's case demonstrates the complexity of this factor, and how individual skills are one aspect of one's overall ability to experience engagement. Although Elosie hasn't become less skilled overall, due to her accident she is not currently able to effectively use skills that had previously come easily. As such, she is underutilized and somewhat at risk for complete disengagement. She recognizes, however, this is just temporary, and as she heals she can begin to be more active.

None of Esme's individual attributes have changed. She is just as skilled as always and has full access to those skills. Unfortunately, her experience of engagement has been impacted by external pressures, things she has very little control over.

The employee/work engagement literature often emphasizes the importance of job resources. Bakker and Demerouti's (2007) job demands-resources theory has consistently shown an important link between work engagement and access to resources. According to Bakker and Demerouti, "job resources refer to those physical, psychological, social, or organizational aspects of the job that may ... (a) be functional in achieving work goals; (b) reduce job demands at the associated physiological and psychological costs; (c) stimulate personal growth and development" (p. 504). Although job resources may be further separated by organization (e.g., compensation, security), relationships (e.g., workplace culture), and characteristics (e.g., role, performance) the perhaps narrow focus on the paid work role may largely ignore other contextual factors that may impede an individual's ability to be engaged at work.

In Esme's case, she has diminished capacity in her work role due to lack of access to needed resources. This is, perhaps, not a surprise; globally, underfunded schools often mean teachers, and students, are trying to do more with less. If, to save money, districts cut staff instead of budgets for supplies, this simply results in a different type of resource (i.e., teachers or support workers) that is no longer available (The Secret Teacher, 2017). As a teacher, Esme's sudden need to redo many lessons plans requires time she does not have. Concurrently, home life has gotten far more complicated due to Elosie's accident. With fewer supports and a greater number of tasks to accomplish, her level of challenge has now exceeded her available capacity, resulting in a move out of the zone of engagement toward feeling overwhelmed.

Time is an interesting resource that can be critically important in optimizing career engagement. As famed management consultant, Peter Drucker, once noted "Everything requires time. It is the one truly universal condition. All work takes place in time and uses up time" (as cited by Aeon & Aguinis, 2017, p. 310). As time is constant, the only way for Esme to *create* more time (i.e., build capacity) to accomplish all her tasks is to set something aside. Her 24-hour day, 7-day week is finite—to make space for more tasks, she needs to set aside something else, perhaps at work (e.g., coaching, tutoring, redoing lesson plans), at home (e.g., laundry, cleaning), or giving up some of her sleep, which could, of course, sacrifice her health. This complex decision about which high-priority activity to set aside is a decision only Esme can make.

Resources are interconnected; changes in one type of resource can impact others, even having a cascading effect where the ultimate outcome is uncertain. For example, if Esme stops tutoring, those students may lose the additional educational support they need to be successful; poor educational outcomes can, in turn, have long lasting impact. This is where it can be critically important to remember that some resources are within the control of the individual, but others might be managed by the employer or another external stakeholder/system (e.g., community, government) over which the individual has very little control. Teachers reacting to budget cuts by buying their own supplies are individual responses to a systemic problem in educational funding. Some teachers may have the resources and make the personal choice to self-fund the supplies they need. Others, however, are either unwilling or unable to pay for needed supplies; some may contribute their time and energy as alternate resources, focused on advocating for change.

Applying Career Engagement

In considering the career engagement model, just a short time before the situations described in the vignette introducing Elosie and Esme in this chapter, both would have described themselves as fully engaged in all aspects of their lives. There were always ebbs and flows, good days and bad, but overall they had established a routine that worked.

For the moment, Elosie is not overly concerned, although she admits to feeling a bit underutilized given her inability to work or to contribute to any of their major household projects. She recognizes, however, that she must focus on healing and supporting Esme as best she can. As time goes on, depending on when Elosie can go back to work, she may start to feel bored; however, she knows the importance of monitoring how she is feeling and, ideally, before moving into feeling fully disengaged, Elosie can begin to take on small projects as her health allows. This can be a delicate balance; taking on too much, too quickly could set back her healing, moving her quite quickly from underutilized to overwhelmed.

Esme, meanwhile, is feeling completely overwhelmed. School budget cuts mean she must rework all her lesson plans, and potentially dip into her savings to ensure her students don't lose out. There are simply not enough resources at work to give her students the education she feels they deserve. If she isn't supplying students with pens, pencils, and art supplies, it is families that are bringing everything from writing paper and glue to tissues and hand sanitizer. Yet, Esme is painfully aware that some of her families can barely afford the essentials and certainly cannot be expected to supplement school supplies.

Home life is not much better for Esme right now. As a couple, Esme and Elosie had divided household chores fairly evenly based on their skills/talents, along with their likes and dislikes. They had really worked hard to fall into a routine that allowed them to be their best selves, as individuals, and as a couple. Now, however, everything is falling to Esme. She loves her job as a teacher and puts in a lot of extra hours and doesn't know how to do less for her students, especially when dealing with budget cuts. She simply and strongly believes her students are worth it. Now, however, she also has Elosie to worry about, ensuring she is resting when she needs to and not doing more than she should, but the more Esme sets aside the more Elosie will try to pick up and do. As a result, Esme is trying to do her work, all her usual household chores, and also all the things Elosie would typically do such as washing cars, mowing the lawn, and doing the laundry.

Ultimately Esme and Elosie recognized that the resources they had available were not only interconnected but could change depending on the week and the role. As Elosie's injuries healed, she needed Esme less and could do more—both of which replenished Esme's capacity. The knowledge that Elosie would be back to full health at some point also helped; they both knew there would soon be an end to the added burden on Esme. They also worked together to be more realistic about priorities and agreed to temporarily delay or contract out things like washing the cars and cutting the grass that they'd normally prided themselves as being on top of.

Activities

5.1   Resource Mapping: Taking Stock

Within the career engagement model, resources are part of capacity and can include a wide range of items that people can use to help offset the challenges they encounter, helping them remain in the zone of engagement. It is important to consider resources in the broadest of terms. Often, resources include the equipment, tools, or supplies needed to get a job done, but time and people can be resources too.

Here is an example from Elosie and Esme.

Although it took *time*, another valuable resource that neither Elosie nor Esme felt they had to give, they began to take stock of all the resources they could reasonably access to help get them through this difficult period. Their goal was to ensure that Elosie had time to heal, and didn't feel guilty taking that time, and that Esme wouldn't burn out or get sick as she took on extra work both at school and at home.

People	External Supports	Notes
Jim and Judy: neighbors		Check to see if they are okay with hiring Markus
Markus: teenage son of Jim and Judy		Mow lawn??
	DoorDash/Uber Eats	Ordering in reduces burden on cooking
	Grocery delivery	Minimize trips to grocery store

Now it's your turn.

People	External Supports	Notes

5.2   Weekly Life/Role Priorities

Esme and Elosie also decided to take time every Sunday evening to set priorities for each week across the roles they were juggling. This allowed them to, together, decide what would be most important to accomplish, what might be nice to get done, and what could reasonably be set aside that week while also ensuring they didn't neglect each other during this busy time. They agreed to post their weekly life role priorities (adapted from Neault, 2010) list on the fridge. Items of highest priority are marked with a 1, those a little less important are marked with a 2; anything with a zero is a low priority item.

Week:							
Major Roles	**Sunday**	**Monday**	**Tuesday**	**Wednesday**	**Thursday**	**Friday**	**Saturday**
Esme: Teaching	1 Prep lesson plan	1 Work	1 Work	1 Personal leave; Elosie physio	1 Work	1 Work	1
Elosie: Home	1 Order Groceries	1 Contact neighbor re: lawn	1 Order dinner	1 Physio	0	0	0
Home-owners	1 Water garden	0	0	0	1 Water garden		1 Mow lawn
Personal Well-being	1 Go for a walk	0	2 Yoga (online)	0	0	0	1 Dinner and a movie

Now it's your turn.

1. At the beginning of each week, identify five or six life roles that will demand most of your attention.
2. For each day of the week, identify the priority that each listed role will have in terms of your time, with a 1 for the highest priority, a 2 for lower priority items, and a 0 for items of lowest priority or that can be completely set aside. Note: This doesn't imply that your overall priorities change daily. It does, however, reflect the reality that on some days your time will be spent more on one important role than another (i.e., a work or school project is due, a child has a birthday, a spouse has medical treatments, a parent is hospitalized).

3. Allocate a dedicated portion of time each week to focus attention on each of the priority roles.

Week:							
Major Roles	**Sunday**	**Monday**	**Tuesday**	**Wednesday**	**Thursday**	**Friday**	**Saturday**
....	....	....	....	....	....	....	....
....	....	....	....	....	....	....	....
....	....	....	....	....	....	....	....
....	....	....	....	....	....	....	....
....	....	....	....	....	....	....	....
....	....	....	....	....	....	....	....
....	....	....	....	....	....	....	....
....	....	....	....	....	....	....	....
....	....	....	....	....	....	....	....
....	....	....	....	....	....	....	....
....	....	....	....	....	....	....	....
....	....	....	....	....	....	....	....
....	....	....	....	....	....	....	....
....	....	....	....	....	....	....	....
....	....	....	....	....	....	....	....
....	....	....	....	....	....	....	....

Five Big Ideas

1. **Think big.** Remember that resources are not limited to equipment or tools. When taking stock of your resources, it is important to think broadly about all the items or things you can access, the skills you have in your tool kit, the people in your life, various community services, and the time you can reasonably give.
2. **Know what you can, and cannot, take on.** Consider your time and personal health and well-being as precious resources. Know when you have more time and energy to commit to projects and when you may need to scale back. Pay attention to the early warning signs of being either overwhelmed or underutilized and adjust accordingly, before things spiral out of control.
3. **Ask for help.** Coworkers, supervisors/managers, schools, family, friends, and community members are all valuable resources. Ask for the help you need and accept the help that is offered; this is not a sign of weakness but a sign of strength. In this, be willing to let go of some control and trust that your helpers will complete their tasks.
4. **Resources are interconnected** and can be dependent on a variety of factors. Our individual ability to access needed resources can be directly related to the capacity of others. Our resources can be depleted simply because we need to find time/energy to support someone else's loss of capacity.
5. **Resources can be fragile and finite.** Life in the 21st century for many people has them living to the margins, leaving little space around day-to-day activities for rest or to accommodate emergencies. When every moment of every day is booked, there is no wiggle room; there may not even appear to be time to access additional resources or to negotiate shifts in timelines or priorities. Leave some white space in the margins of your life!

References

Aeon, B., & Aguinis, H. (2017). It's about time: New perspectives and insights on time management. *Academy of Management Perspectives, 31*, 309–330. https://doi.org/10.5465/amp.2016.0166

Bakker, A. B., & Demerouti, E. (2007). The job demands-resources model: State of the art. *Journal of Managerial Psychology, 22*(3), 309–328. https://doi.org/10.1108/02683940710733115

Csikszentmihalyi, M. (1990). *Flow: The psychology of optimal experience.* Harper & Row.

Neault, R. A. (2006). *Career strategies for a lifetime of success.* Life Strategies.

Neault, R. (2010). *That elusive work-life balance* (2nd ed). Life Strategies.

The Secret Teacher. (2017, November 11). Secret Teacher: I don't have the equipment and resources to do my job. *The Guardian.* https://www.theguardian.com/teacher-network/2017/nov/11/secret-teacher-equipment-or-resources-to-do-my-job-funding-cuts

Figure Credit

IMG 5.1: Copyright © 2014 Depositphotos/MilicaC.

CHAPTER SIX

Capacity: Relationships

OPENING VIGNETTE

IMG. 6.1

Sadie was proud of her First Nations heritage. She had lived in the same northern community all her life and was surrounded, all day, every day, by members of her family and also friends with whom she'd grown up. Sadie had done well in the band-operated village school and then completed a social work degree online, with very high grades. For as long as she can remember, her goal had been to work in the band offices to help her people, especially children and families. Throughout high school and university, Sadie worked part-time in after-school community programs for children and youth. She was loved and respected by everyone she worked with—the children, their families, her coworkers, and her supervisors.

Once Sadie graduated with her social work degree, however, the nature of her work and some of her relationships with friends, family, and community members began to change. Although she'd certainly heard of discrimination against Indigenous peoples, that hadn't been her day-to-day reality. However, now that her work took her into meetings in the city with other professionals, she began to witness what her clients and family members had been describing to her. The beliefs held by city professionals about the people from her village were absolutely astounding to her—and incredibly hurtful. Her people were generally viewed as uneducated, unmotivated, irresponsible, abusive, and lawbreakers. This broke Sadie's heart; those weren't accurate descriptions of the people she knew so well and loved so deeply.

Sadly, those beliefs also led to discriminatory actions. Some of her young clients were arrested when similar incidents with non-Indigenous youth would have resulted in only a warning or a report to the youth's parents, who would then be given sole responsibility for correcting the problem. Each day Sadie heard arguments for removing a child from parental care, resulting often in foster care placements outside of the community. Although there had been changes in recent years, focusing more on keeping children with their parents or within their extended families, Sadie witnessed that "old habits die hard" and, among many of her professional colleagues, the go-to solution was still to apprehend a child.

Aside from these clear cases of discrimination against her clients and community, Sadie's relationships with some of her family and friends also started to change. Although she didn't think she was that different, others began to be intimidated by her degree, new responsibilities at work, and even the words she used when talking with them. Some people simply avoided her or talked behind her back; others told her that she just didn't seem like the same Sadie that they'd always known and loved. Some of Sadie's family and friends refuse to acknowledge her responsibilities to her employer, expecting that there will be exceptions to the rules due to Sadie's newly influential role. Within the community relationships matter—as they do at work—and there's an apparently irreconcilable tension between her key roles.

Sadie's supervisor, Carol, on the other hand, was an amazing resource to her. The social work program that Sadie had graduated from had a formal mentorship program for the first 3 years post-graduation. Although mentors could be assigned by the program coordinator, they strongly recommended that a local mentor who had similar personal and professional experiences would be the best fit. Sadie's supervisor, Carol, agreed to serve in this special role; she, too, had previously graduated from the same program and had found working with her own mentor to be what kept her grounded on the most difficult days.

Exploring the Factor: Relationships

Within the career engagement model, one of the factors contributing to capacity is *relationships*. Of course, many significant relationships are personal ones—parents, spouses, siblings, friends, teachers, children, extended family members, teammates, and others with whom we interact regularly. In the workplace, key relationships might be with coworkers, supervisors, and managers. In some roles, like Sadie's, important relationships might also include clients, community members, and professional colleagues. Some individuals also work with mentors or coaches. Sadie is thrilled to have her supervisor play the dual role of her professional mentor.

As Sadie's story illustrates, however, even positive relationships can shift over time. Although Sadie's professional roles within the band office are all positive, and she is appreciated by most of her clients and their families, she is struggling to fit in with professional colleagues from the city and is experiencing tension with some of her family members and longtime friends.

Racial discrimination surrounds us. A relatively recent acronym (BIPOC: Black, Indigenous, and people of color) has become an umbrella term for many groups impacted by the resurgence of race-related hate crimes. Even, as in Sadie's case, when one isn't directly the target of discrimination and hate crimes, witnessing racial discrimination at work can negatively impact organizational commitment (Ragins et al., 2017), and commitment to one's organization is an element of many employee engagement models (e.g., Neault & Pickerell, 2011).

Ragins et al. (2017) particularly focused on the buffering or anchoring effect of mentors who had high-quality relationships with their mentees such as Sadie's supervisor/

mentor had with Sadie. In this research, mentees were less likely to lose organizational commitment than their colleagues who didn't have effective mentors. It was interesting, however, that a similar effect wasn't found in general relationships with coworkers or typical supervisors. An exception to this was in relationships where supervisors served in a dual role as mentors; supervisor-mentors who formed positive supportive relationships with their mentees served as buffers from the stress-related impacts of witnessing discrimination and also served to retain employees within the organization. This research highlights the value of access to strong and supportive mentors within the workplace, especially in the midst of discrimination. Given the current global context acknowledging a rise in racially inspired hate crimes and workplace inequities that continue to be experienced by BIPOC individuals, it may be more important than ever for organizations that want to maximize the career engagement of their employees to invest in mentors. In Sadie's case, her supportive relationship with her supervisor/mentor has kept her from quitting her job.

McKeown and Ayoko (2020) emphasized the importance of supervisory and coworker relationships to an employee's experience of thriving at work, which could be considered similar to career engagement. Although, as previously mentioned, Ragins et al. (2017) noted that supervisors and coworkers can't generally mitigate the negative outcomes from witnessing racial discrimination at work, McKeown and Ayoko highlighted the key positive roles that coworkers and supervisors *can* play in contributing to employees' career engagement and general life satisfaction.

In some industries, employees are at higher risk of being exposed to disrespect and incivility (McKeown & Ayoko, 2020) and this, too, can impact career engagement. As McKeown and Ayoka highlighted, relationships at work *do* matter. Positive and supportive coworker, supervisor, and mentor relationships can buffer and mitigate the impact of stress-inducing experiences that, if unaddressed, could lead to employee disengagement, absenteeism, and decisions to leave the organization.

In other research, Haar et al. (2019) investigated whether positive work relationships impacted employees' perception of work being meaningful; this bridges the career engagement components of challenge and capacity, with *meaningful opportunities* being a challenge factor in our model and *relationships* being a capacity factor.

The research of Haar et al. (2019) illustrates and reconfirms the interconnectedness of the factors contributing to engagement. To a certain extent, categorization is arbitrary. It's the interaction between all these factors that contributes to one achieving and sustaining engagement at work and across the complexity of life roles. In their research within a group of managers in New Zealand, Haar et al. found that positive relationships at work (i.e., relationships characterized by mutual respect, caring, and connectedness between managers and subordinates) contributed to manager happiness, greater well-being, and work engagement and performance. Interestingly, however, these findings were stronger within larger organizations with "high-quality" staff (p. 12). This suggests that positive workplace relationships, especially between managers and subordinates, may impact employee engagement differently in large organizations than in small ones; there may also be relationship impact differences between workplaces with predominantly professional/technical employees as compared to those with a less educated, more entry-level workforce. In Sadie's case, her positive relationships with her supervisor, coworkers, clients, and their families have contributed to keeping her work both meaningful and motivating. In career engagement language, Sadie's positive relationships contribute to her capacity to meet the daily challenges of working with her complex client caseload and the ambient discrimination surrounding her work.

Applying Career Engagement

Sadie had always had strong, positive relationships with her immediate and extended family, lifelong friends, community, and colleagues at work. It felt so foreign to her to have some of the people she'd spent her lifetime with turn against her because of her new position and responsibilities at work. When she'd started her new job, Sadie would have identified herself on the career engagement model as optimally engaged. Her work was challenging (both motivating and meaningful), her education had prepared her well for it, and she had a good balance of work and other life roles that didn't feel overwhelming.

However, as she became more established within her new role, Sadie began to witness the discrimination that she'd previously been quite sheltered from—and it was traumatizing to her. She began to lose sleep at night, feeling powerless to protect her clients. Perhaps even more upsetting, Sadie felt blindsided by losing previously close relationships with several of her friends and family members. Those relationships, and her place within the community, were important to her. Feeling isolated and disrespected by people she cared about hurt her and made her wonder if she could continue to work in her new profession.

Sadie found herself moving out of the zone of engagement and beginning to feel overwhelmed. However, when she imagined herself quitting her job, that didn't seem like a good solution either. She was sure she'd be bored in no time and didn't want to waste her education and just hang out with her friends and family, losing her sense of purpose and contribution.

Sadie's supervisor, Carol, who also served as her mentor, played a key role in helping Sadie to navigate this challenging time at work and in the community. One of the key advantages, aside from their closeness, mutual respect, and deep trust, was that the supervisor had previously walked along a very similar path. She understood the impact of vicarious trauma and was able to help Sadie access counseling and begin to engage in some self-care activities. As a result, Sadie started sleeping better again and was able to reframe her focus on the positive accomplishments that she was witnessing every day rather than solely on what was unjust or going wrong.

Sadie's supervisor/mentor was also instrumental in helping her understand the changes in her personal relationships. Sadie learned to focus on the relationships that were most precious to her and to find ways to reopen positive communication and to engage in activities that emphasized commonalities rather than differences, helping her close family and friends to understand that she was still the same Sadie inside.

Relationships are important to all of us. Within the career engagement model, they can serve as personal and professional resources, bolstering our capacity and equipping us to handle our most challenging moments.

Activities

6.1 Relationships Matter

Reflect on relationships that are important to you, at work or in school, as well as in your personal life. Consider both what's working well (the strengths of the relationship) and what's not working well (your struggles). After completing the table, choose two positive relationships to focus on to strengthen even more. Choose one or two relationships that are currently a struggle but important enough to you to rebuild. Write specific actions that you can take as first steps for each of these priority relationships (adapted from Neault, 2012).

As an example, here's Sadie's chart and action plan.

Who?	What's Working?	What's Not?
Carol (supervisor/ mentor)	She really "gets" me; we spend 15 minutes each day chatting and go for one longer lunch each week.	
Mom	Always encouraging; proud of my degree and my job with the band	
Jenny (cousin)		Seems jealous; has stopped visiting; I've heard from others that she thinks I think I'm better than all of them now ☹
Tim (social worker in city)	Seems to like me as a colleague and treats my opinions with respect	He's constantly badmouthing my people; doesn't seem to get how hurtful that is (and that I'm one of them, too!)

Making good relationships better:

Who?	How?
Carol	Start to keep a journal of the discrimination I see and of the accomplishments that I've contributed to so that we have specific things to focus on when we meet
Tim	Invite him to join me at a professional development event about the impact of residential schools on our community

Getting struggling relationships back on track:

Who?	How?
Jenny	Invite Jenny to join me at a community event; try to spend time just with her at least once each week
Tim	Consider offering to do a presentation through the local professional association on the personal impact of "ambient discrimination" and "vicarious trauma"; Tim always attends those events. Perhaps then we could talk about my experiences with both of those over coffee one day?

Now it's your turn.

Who?	What's Working?	What's Not?

Who?	What's Working?	What's Not?
. . . .	. . . .	. . . .
. . . .	. . . .	. . . .
. . . .	. . . .	. . . .
. . . .	. . . .	. . . .
. . . .	. . . .	. . . .
. . . .	. . . .	. . . .
. . . .	. . . .	. . . .
. . . .	. . . .	. . . .
. . . .	. . . .	. . . .
. . . .	. . . .	. . . .
. . . .	. . . .	. . . .
. . . .	. . . .	. . . .
. . . .	. . . .	. . . .
. . . .	. . . .	. . . .
. . . .	. . . .	. . . .
. . . .	. . . .	. . . .

Making good relationships better:

Who?	How?
. . . .	. . . .
. . . .	. . . .
. . . .	. . . .
. . . .	. . . .

Who?	How?
. . . .	. . . .
. . . .	. . . .
. . . .	. . . .
. . . .	. . . .
. . . .	. . . .
. . . .	. . . .
. . . .	. . . .
. . . .	. . . .
. . . .	. . . .
. . . .	. . . .
. . . .	. . . .
. . . .	. . . .
. . . .	. . . .
. . . .	. . . .
. . . .	. . . .
. . . .	. . . .

Getting struggling relationships back on track:

Who?	How?
. . . .	. . . .
. . . .	. . . .
. . . .	. . . .
. . . .	. . . .

Who?	How?
....	....
....	....
....	....
....	....
....	....
....	....
....	....
....	....
....	....
....	....
....	....
....	....
....	....
....	....
....	....
....	....

Adapted from Roberta Neault, *Career Strategies for a Lifetime of Success*. Copyright © 2012 by Life Strategies Ltd. Reprinted with permission.

6.2   Synergy: When Two Are Stronger Than One

There's an old saying that "the whole is greater than the sum of its parts." That means that there are things we can accomplish together that we wouldn't be able to accomplish if working independently, even if we were working toward the same goal. Think of a project that you're working on or would like to accomplish. Identify at least one other person to help you with it—even better would be to build a team of three or more. Identify three action steps you could take as you begin to introduce your idea to others and to invite them to join you on your project.

Here's an example from Sadie.

My project idea:

Cleaning out and replanting the community garden, teaching children and youth about traditional plants for food and medicine.

Who?	How might they contribute?
Auntie Kathy	She has such a green thumb; she'll know how to prepare the ground for planting
Elders (e.g., JT)	As knowledge keepers, they can share stories of traditional plants and their purposes
Jenny	I'm looking for projects to work on with her to rebuild our friendship; she'll enjoy getting some of the kids in the community involved
Sunshine Nursery	A business in the local town known for supporting youth projects; if we can demonstrate how this will involve children and youth, they will likely contribute some planters, soil, fertilizer, seeds, and plants

Now it's your turn.

My project idea:

Who?	How might they contribute?

Who?	How might they contribute?
....	....
....	....
....	....
....	....
....	....

6.3 When You Hurt, I Hurt: Vicarious Trauma

When we care about people, when they hurt, we hurt, too. There are examples all around us of discrimination, race-based hate crimes, and injustice. Create a collage of 10-plus headlines or photos with captions about how your clients, colleagues, community members, or other people you care about are portrayed in the media. Then, write a brief reflection (bullet points or key words are fine) about how the collage impacts your career engagement (e.g., Do you feel overwhelmed? Beyond caring? Energized to do something to change things?).

Here's Sadie's example.

> I created a collage of headlines and photos from the local newspaper involving various people from my own community. I won't include it here as it identifies people by name and, even though it was drawn from public sources, I don't want to victimize them twice. However, when I looked at the images and words I'd collected, they were almost entirely negative, and it made me incredibly sad. Although I feel a bit overwhelmed, I can also see how my work in the community is already making a difference. Through my relationships here, I've helped to find jobs for some of our youth—and, in our nearby city, the arrests of youth from our community have gone down by 20% this year. As I build more connections with employers and community leaders, gain (or regain) trust with my family and friends in the community, and engage others in the community in projects like the community garden, I think I'll begin to feel more engaged than overwhelmed again. It's challenging for sure, but that's what makes this work important!

And now it's your turn. Create the collage on paper, poster board, or your computer or tablet. Space for your reflection is provided.

....

....

....

....

....

Five Big Ideas

1. **Relationships are complex, multidimensional, and interconnected.** Especially within small communities, your personal and professional relationships may intersect in multiple ways. Relationships may be mutually beneficial, mutually destructive, or concurrently helpful and hurtful.
2. **Relationships evolve.** Some relationships drift apart naturally. Others are critically important to maintain and, when ruptured, need your intentional effort (e.g., time, energy, resources) to repair them.
3. **Nurture your network.** Professional and personal networks serve as important resources. They strengthen your capacity to handle the challenges life and work bring your way.
4. **Relationships can be synergistic.** In effective teams or partnerships, "the sum of the whole is greater than the sum of the parts." Seek out complementary relationships and experience the magic of working together.
5. **Mentorship matters.** A strong mentoring relationship can offer a buffer from stress, vicarious trauma, and overly challenging work/life experiences. Find a mentor for yourself. Be a mentor to others.

References

Haar, J., Schmitz, A., Di Fabio, A., & Daellenbach, U. (2019). The role of relationships at work and happiness: A moderated moderated mediation study of New Zealand managers. *Sustainability (Basel, Switzerland)*, 11(12), 3443. https://doi.org/10.3390/su11123443

McKeown, T., & Ayoko, O. B. (2020). Relationships at work—why do they matter so much? *Journal of Management & Organization, 26*(2), 133–134. https://doi.org/10.1017/jmo.2020.3

Neault, R. (2012). *Career strategies for a lifetime of success* (3rd ed.). Life Strategies.

Neault, R. A., & Pickerell, D. A. (2011). Career engagement: Bridging career counseling and employee engagement. *Journal of Employment Counseling, 48*(4), 185–188. https://doi.org/10.1002/j.2161-1920.2011.tb01111.x

Ragins, B. R., Ehrhardt, K., Lyness, K. S., Murphy, D. D., & Capman, J. F. (2017). Anchoring relationships at work: High-quality mentors and other supportive work relationships as buffers to ambient racial discrimination. *Personnel Psychology, 70*(1), 211–256. https://doi.org/10.1111/peps.12144

Figure Credit

CHAPTER SEVEN

Capacity: Workload

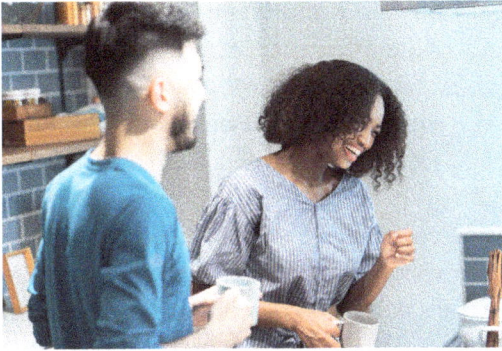

IMG. 7.1

Born in Lagos, Nigeria, Daraja and her family came to Canada when she was just 8 years old, under the economic class entry visa, settling in Stratford, a small community outside of Toronto in Ontario. Now, at 35, Daraja has followed in her father's footsteps, working as a radiation oncologist at Toronto's Mount Sinai Hospital. Married for just 3 years, her husband, Jian, is a second-generation Chinese Canadian working as a clinical research associate with a focus in applied genomics. Daraja is only a month into her maternity leave, after the birth of twin sons.

Daraja and Jian have demanding jobs, something they have never minded. They both worked incredibly hard to get where they are in their careers and know they are doing critically important work—work that truly can, and does, save lives. Neither minded that work seemed to never "turn off." Checking emails, responding to messages, and taking calls during evenings, weekends, and even on vacation was never a problem.

Things changed, however, after the birth of the twins. Daraja got quite used to being away from work and, although she missed patients and colleagues and the crazy hospital life, adjusting to life as a new mother presented a whole new set of challenges. Jian had tried to scale back work, to give him more time with his sons, but also found it hard to change old habits, even while recognizing he was missing out on so much.

It has become quite clear to both that they want to keep growing their careers but that they do need to change how they manage that aspect of their lives in order to also be the kind of parents they've always dreamed of being.

Exploring the Factor: Workload

Workload is another factor within the *capacity* component of the career engagement model and is an important element within the broader employee/work engagement literature. Maslach et al.'s (2001) job engagement model specifically addresses *sustainable* workload. Similarly, Bakker and Demerouti's (2007) job demands-resources theory includes workload as a job demand. The burnout-antithesis approach (Maslach et al., 2001) also considered workload a component of exhaustion, which is one of three burnout dimensions.

According to Byrne, workload is "the feeling of having excessive role demands given the time and various resources available to address them" (as cited by Montani et al., 2020, p. 60). The inclusion of the demands of specific roles is important, as it acknowledges, at least to some degree, the existence of nonpaid work roles and the subsequent demands these place on individuals. Unfortunately, much of the employee/work engagement literature is focused solely on paid work, seeming to ignore lives outside of the workplace. Yet, there is a body of literature that connects workload to role theory, which connects to role stress and, of course, role overload.

Separate from Byrne's original definition, within the career engagement model workload is not necessarily *excessive*; instead, it simply acknowledges that there may be multiple demands an individual is juggling (i.e., their "load") across various life roles. Though the original research into the career engagement model focused on the paid work role, it was not at the expense of other roles that may affect opportunities to maximize engagement. This is where Byrne's definition of workload connects to our work. The impact on individuals of nonpaid work roles, which may include parent, child, spouse/partner, caregiver, student, and volunteer, among many others, must not be overlooked. Participation in work and nonwork roles changes over time, as does the salience or importance of each role.

Stevenson and Duxbury (2019) noted that Kahn and his colleagues, back in 1964, "were the first to empirically define and ratify role overload as a time-based form of inter-role or intra-role stress" (p. 330). They cited numerous studies demonstrating that role overload is a serious problem with many consequences, including poorer physical and mental health and well-being, increased absenteeism and intent to leave, diminished productivity, and greater instances of family distress.

Role overload is defined as "the perception that the demands imposed by a single or multiple roles are so great that time and energy resources are not sufficient to fulfill the requirements of the roles to the satisfaction of one's self or others" (Duxbury et al., 2018, p. 250). Much has been written about work role overload, family role overload and how these combine to total role overload, along with work-to-family and family-to-work conflict and various gender implications, though this latter piece is somewhat underrepresented (Babic & Hansez, 2021; Duxbury et al., 2018; Recuero & Segovia, 2021).

This is reflected in Daraja and Jian's case. Although leading busy, full lives they had found a balance between their paid roles and their roles as spouses and, given both sets of parents are in good health, to a lesser extent their roles as children. Then, however, the twins arrived, and with them, the need to embrace and prioritize their roles as parents.

Applying Career Engagement

Workload is another factor within the capacity component of the career engagement model. As noted in the previous section, "work" extends beyond one's paid role to include a variety of other roles and their associated tasks and activities. The broad goal should be to experience career engagement across all facets of life; it is not a state reserved solely for the employed. In considering interventions, however, it can be beneficial to focus on one role at a time, generally starting with the one that seems of greatest concern.

For many years, Daraja and Jian have felt fully engaged across their busy lives. They will admit, however, that work pressures often had them feeling somewhat overwhelmed. None of those pressures were cause for major concern. Any movement out of the zone of engagement was slight, and often easily corrected.

For Daraja, her pregnancy and delivery could not have been smoother; for that she feels quite blessed. Being a new mother is an interesting dual-engagement experience, especially once Jian returned to work after a brief parental leave. Daraja often felt unprepared for the challenges two new babies bring. The tasks of feeding, changing, comforting, and caring for her boys were both motivating and meaningful (the two factors that comprise the challenge component) but, in some cases, seemed more difficult than she had anticipated. One of the twins was colicky, requiring more attention and, overall, she just never seemed to have time to get everything done that she had hoped to accomplish. All the tasks she was juggling as a mother and primary caregiver were overwhelming, especially given her limited capacity, more specifically time, energy, and supports; she just felt continually exhausted. Jian was doing his best, but his job was demanding, and he was gone for a huge chunk of the day.

At the same time, Daraja was missing her work colleagues and patients. She clearly loved her children and cherished this time with them but also craved intellectual stimulation. When considering her work role, which was important but not a primary role at this time, she felt quite underutilized.

Jian was also struggling to maximize engagement, but his individual context made the experience quite different. Being back at work, Jian was completely immersed with the challenge his paid work role presented. His work was important; it meant a great deal to him. There were times, however, he found his mind wandering as he thought about what Daraja and the twins were doing. He truly has no words for what it feels like to be a new father and was amazed at how the twins were changing, seemingly every day. He worried about what he might be missing.

It was, however, when he got home that he felt overwhelmed. He could tell Daraja was exhausted and often felt guilty about what did not get done. To try to alleviate the pressure, Jian would jump in with whatever needed doing: laundry, cooking, cleaning, caring for the twins. They would try to get the twins to bed early, hoping to spend quality time together but, too often, would find themselves using their evenings to catch up and try to prepare for the next day; plus, Jian always spent at least an hour answering work emails. Prior to the twins, this was never an issue, but work interfering with home life was getting increasingly problematic.

Ultimately Daraja and Jian recognized they needed to make a change. They were feeling overwhelmed and stressed far too often, causing increased tension. Over time they were confident things would not seem so challenging at home, but they needed to do something now. At first, neither were certain how to reduce the challenge; parenthood was not always easy. They could, however, look at ways to build capacity.

First, Jian rearranged his work calendar, blocking off an hour each morning and afternoon to deal with email. He also informed his team, and his supervisor, that he was no longer going to spend time at night, or on weekends, attending to work. Everyone at work was fully supportive; realistically, no one expected him, or anyone else, to work during their personal time. It just somehow happened. In any case, with this extra time at night, it was decided that Jian would take over bedtime routine, giving him some quality time with his sons and letting Daraja have a break.

Together, they agreed that, through the week especially, it truly didn't matter if dishes weren't dried and put away or if laundry wasn't folded, or even done. It seemed to be an unwritten "rule" that had worked before the twins but now just seemed so trivial. Daraja needed to rest when the twins rested, at least until they were sleeping better at night. They also spoke to both sets of parents about ways they could be more involved through the week. They had always offered, but Daraja had, at first, been determined to do it all on her own. However, she realized that she had access to these amazing resources in her parents and in-laws and, in giving herself permission to not waste time doing less important tasks, she had added capacity and was able to spend more time feeling energized and engaged.

Activities

7.1   Jar of Rocks[1]

There are many activities that can help sort priorities,[2] but one popular metaphor is a jar of rocks with various priorities being big rocks (the most important), smaller rocks or pebbles (important, but can be set aside), and sand (lowest priority but still takes up space). A quick trip to any craft store, or perhaps the beach, can likely secure these items, bringing the metaphor to life. However, for now, a worksheet works.

Daraja and Jian could do this activity separately but have, instead, decided to focus on their joint role as parents.

---

1   This is a popular model to discuss time and priorities. It is described in various ways on the internet and vaguely attributed to "a philosophy professor" or a "time management expert."

2   See Chapter 5 for a weekly life-role priorities worksheet.

Our big rocks:

Each other and the twins

Our pebbles:

Our families: important for the twins to have a good relationship with their grandparents

Our careers: we've worked too hard to set these aside, but we do need to consider how our careers may evolve over time. We also need to recognize that we likely can't grow our careers concurrently and some opportunities may need to be overlooked until the twins are older.

The sand in our lives:

Everything else, including the hunt for a bigger home. For now, this can wait.

Now it's your turn.

My big rocks:

....

....

....

....

....

....

My pebbles:

....

....

....

....

The sand in my life:

....

....

_____

....

....

_____

....

....

_____

7.2   Managing Time and Tasks

Daraja and Jian found the Eisenhower (n.d.) matrix helpful in sorting out what needed to get done. In working with this framework, it was important to remember they can spend as much time in each quadrant as they want, but how much time they have available, overall, remains constant (i.e., there are exactly 24 hours available each day, regardless of whether that feels like sufficient time to get everything they consider important done). In general, it is suggested that the bulk of time be focused in Quadrant 2, on items that are both important and not urgent. Here is what an Eisenhower matrix looks like.

	Urgent	**Not Urgent**
Important	**Quadrant 1** ● Necessary tasks ● Strive to reduce time here	**Quadrant 2** ● Focus on quality ● Strive to maximize time here
Not Important	**Quadrant 3** ● Manage interruptions ● Seek to delegate or reject	**Quadrant 4** ● Distractions ● Avoid altogether

Daraja and Jian used this matrix regularly, considering daily and sometimes weekly tasks. Here is an example Daraja did for a recent week.

	Urgent	Not Urgent
Important	Researching daycares, giving sufficient lead time to visit and make a decision	Caring for twins
Not Important	Twins' laundry; for Wednesday with grandparents Set up account with grocery delivery and meal delivery services (14-day free trial ends in 10 days).	Giving myself permission to ignore house cleaning and weeding flowerpots

Now it's your turn.

	Urgent	Not Urgent
Important		
Not Important		

Five Big Ideas

1. **Workload is more than paid work.** Although the terms *work* and *workload* may immediately bring paid employment or a job to mind, this factor includes all the activities or tasks that must get done each day, week, or month. From laundry to cleaning and from lessons to self-care, make sure you have a clear picture of all the tasks that are part of your load.

2. **Workload isn't static.** Not only are there regular, or even planned, ebbs and flows, your workload can also change in an instant. An unexpected email or phone call from a child's school can impact everything you had hoped to accomplish. To further complicate matters, shifts in the capacity of others to handle their own load can unexpectedly transfer tasks to you. Someone else's unanticipated emergency can impact their ability to fulfill their responsibilities, forcing you to fill the gap or find other resources.

3. **Beware of the tyranny of the urgent** (Hummel, 1994). There is a difference between items that are urgent but not important and items that are urgent and important. In today's 24/7, respond-immediately lives, it can be hard to remain focused and unbothered by interruptions. As Natalie Goldberg once said, "Nothing is that important. Just lie down" (Goodreads, n.d.).

4. **Self-care isn't selfish.** A cardinal rule when flying is to put on your own oxygen mask before helping others. Yet in so many other areas of life, caregivers are often programmed to put themselves last. You can't possibly carry a full workload if you are not well, whether that is physically, mentally, or emotionally. Always take time for self-care, from exercising and eating right to getting enough sleep and finding time for fun. If you don't put yourself first, at least on occasion, you'll have nothing left for everyone else.

5. **Boundaries are important.** Know when to say no and stand firm. Recognize when you have reached your maximum and cannot take on anything else without risking becoming overwhelmed. Similarly, recognize when you have room to shift, thereby supporting others in their own efforts to optimize career engagement.

References

Babic, A., & Hansez, I. (2021). The glass ceiling for women managers: Antecedents and consequences for work-family interface and well-being at work. *Frontiers in Psychology.* https://doi.org/10.3389/fpsyg.2021.618250

Bakker, A. B., & Demerouti, E. (2007). The job demands-resources model: State of the art. *Journal of Managerial Psychology, 22*(3), 309–328. https://doi.org/10.1108/02683940710733115

Duxbury, L., Stevenson, M., & Higgins, C. (2018). Too much to do, too little time: Role overload and stress in a multi-role environment. *International Journal of Stress Management, 25*(3), 250–266. https://doi.org/10.1037/str0000062

Goodreads. (n.d.). *Quote by Natalie Goldberg.* https://www.goodreads.com/quotes/172780-stress-is-basically-a-disconnection-from-the-earth-a-forgetting

Eisenhower. (n.d.). *Introducing the Eisenhower matrix.* https://www.eisenhower.me/eisenhower-matrix/

Hummell, C. E. (1994). *Tyranny of the urgent.* IVP Books.

Maslach, C., Schaufeli, W. B., & Leiter, M. P. (2001). Job burnout. *Annual Review of Psychology, 52,* 397–422. http://dx.doi.org/10.1146%2Fannurev.psych.52.1.397

Montani, F., Vandenberghe, C., Khedhaouria, A., & Courcy, F. (2020). Examining the inverted U-shaped relationship between workload and innovative work behavior: The role of work engagement and mindfulness. *Human Relations (New York)*, 73(1), 59–93. https://doi.org/10.1177/0018726718819055

Recuero, L. H., & Segovia, A. O. (2021). Work-family conflict, coping strategies and burnout: A gender and couple analysis. *Journal of Work and Organizational Psychology*, 37(1) 21–28. https://doi.org/10.5093/jwop2021a5

Stevenson, M., & Duxbury, L. (2019). Overloaded and stressed: A case study of women working in the health care sector. *Journal of Occupational Health Psychology*, 24(3), 333–345. https://doi.org/10.1037/ocp0000111

Figure Credit

CHAPTER EIGHT

Capacity: Well-Being

IMG. 8.1

Jacquie dreaded going to work these days. The feelings of dread started Sunday evening, and it wasn't until late Saturday afternoon that she started to feel "like herself" again. Normally a happy, generous, optimistic person, both at home and at work, Jacquie rarely smiled now. She had lost the bounce in her step and barely had enough energy to get through the day, picking up fast food on the way home from work, crawling onto the couch as soon as her kids were in bed, and most nights falling asleep there watching TV after working her way through a bottle of wine. She had no interest in fun anymore, had stopped visiting family and friends, and had recently canceled her gym membership as she hadn't been to the gym in months. Jacquie's sister was getting really worried; she finally talked Jacquie into seeing a counselor to help her figure out what had changed and to find a way back to "normal."

Exploring the Factor: Well-Being

A key factor of the capacity component in the career engagement model is well-being. The items that comprise this factor have consistently clustered across much of our early research on the model, although the factor was originally labeled "work–life balance." Our focus on balance and well-being was largely influenced by the extensive work done by Duxbury and Higgins (2003, 2009, 2012), among others, related to work–life conflicts, which acknowledged the ever-increasing complexity seen in today's families (e.g., dual-career couples, single parents, blended families, sandwich generation) and how work and other life roles were often in conflict with one another. More recently, with mental health rates on the rise and a lessening, at least somewhat, of the stigma associated with mental illness/health, there has been some interesting research exploring the interconnectedness of work and mental health (Redekopp &

Huston, 2020), as well as evidence of the relationship between employee well-being and engagement (Bakker & Demerouti, 2008).

In keeping with this ongoing and emerging research, well-being seemed a more appropriate label for this factor, even while recognizing that a single agreed-on definition doesn't exist in the literature (Schulte et al., 2015) and that well-being should perhaps be considered separately from mental health (Burns et al., 2016).

Within the career engagement model, well-being is perhaps most closely aligned to the Gallup-Healthways Wellbeing Index (Schulte et al., 2015) which recognizes five indices: life evaluation (i.e., evaluation of present life experience with what is anticipated 5 years in the future), emotional health (e.g., happiness, anger, depression, life enjoyment), physical health (e.g., quality of sleep, weight, propensity of illness, diagnosed diseases), healthy behavior (e.g., smoking, drinking, exercise), work environment (e.g., job satisfaction and relationship with supervisor), and basic access (i.e., access to health care, clean water, medicine, safe environment to live).

Regardless of approach to, or definition of, well-being, it is becoming clear that a link exists between well-being and various important organizational factors, including performance, productivity, and engagement (Ariza-Montes et al., 2019; Lewis & Donaldson-Feilder, 2014; Rasool et al., 2021). Attending to, and facilitating, individual employees' well-being can mitigate the risk of losing key people to extended medical leaves, quitting their jobs for other less stressful or toxic opportunities, or simply counting their remaining days until retirement.

Applying Career Engagement

Working with a counselor from her workplace's employee assistance program, Jacquie soon recognized that her feelings of dread had begun about a month after her current supervisor had been assigned to her department. At first, Jacquie thought that it would just take some time to build the type of positive relationship that she had enjoyed with her previous supervisor over the past 5 years. The new supervisor was more critical than Jacquie was used to and didn't see himself as part of the team. The only time he came out of his office seemed to be when he was frustrated or angry about something. Jacquie wasn't the only one who tensed up as soon as his door opened. She now found herself second-guessing every action she took and every decision she made, wondering what the supervisor would disagree with next. Being at work used to be fun and engaging; now it was both confusing and discouraging. Jacquie had lost all confidence in her competency to do the job and worried constantly about being fired.

Although Jacquie and her counselor also identified some other key changes in Jacquie's life that might have been contributing to her declining mental health and well-being, the tipping point seemed to be the toxic work environment. The nervousness, uneasiness, and tension Jacquie is feeling likely represents situational workplace anxiety—a transient state tied to specific workplace situa-tions (Cheng & McCarthy, 2018). Unrelenting work-related stress and the resulting anxiety were impacting her ability to be fully engaged with her teenaged children and to be patient with her mom, who had been recently diagnosed with early onset Alzheimer's. In unpacking her various life roles, however, Jacquie soon realized that if she could "get back to normal" at work, then she'd once again have the energy to face other challenges that came her way.

With her counselor, Jacquie explored stressors that were within her control and those that weren't. They also discussed healthy coping resources; although Jacquie already knew about the importance of exercise, getting enough sleep, eating well, and social support, she began to recognize that she'd recently let all the good habits that she'd been building in those areas slip away. She was frustrated that she'd allowed the new supervisor to have such a negative impact on her.

The counselor suggested that Jacquie check in with her physician, in part to rule out any physical causes of her malaise. Jacquie's doctor was very concerned with her decline over the past 6 months and strongly recommended taking some time off work. With a doctor's note in hand, Jacquie made an appointment with her HR advisor the next day and arranged to take a medical leave. Jacquie mentioned the changes that had occurred in her department; the HR advisor didn't seem to be surprised, as others had also reported similar concerns.

The career engagement model emphasizes the importance of aligning challenge and capacity. Challenge, as discussed earlier in the book, comprises both meaning-ful opportunities and motivating work. Although the work itself hadn't changed, Jacquie's toxic work environment had impacted both aspects of challenge; she was no longer able to engage with the tasks that she found most meaningful and, with constant anxiety about her supervisor's reactions, she'd lost the motivation to be innovative and productive. Concurrently, Jacquie had less capacity; she'd lost several key supportive relationships, including her previous supervisor, collegial conversa-tions at work, and time with her family and friends. Her workload felt unmanageable and hopeless as nothing she did seemed to be good enough for her supervisor. Over time, she'd given up any semblance of a healthy lifestyle, increasing her drinking, eating nothing but fast food, and sprawling on the couch at night rather than going to the gym.

Jacquie worked with her physician and counselor to plan for a successful return to work. Her first focus, all agreed, had to be on rebuilding her health, emotional well-being, and resilience. Jacquie hadn't realized how completely exhausted she was; for the 1st week off work, she had little energy for anything but sleep. However, by the 2nd week, she was beginning to have a bit more energy and noticed that her jumpiness had diminished. She was ready to build some health and fitness activities back into her life. Before renewing her gym membership, Jacquie agreed to start walking each day, spending at least 30 minutes in the fresh air. She agreed to track her food intake for 1 week and then to gradually begin to make healthier choices for snacks and meals. Without even trying, she noticed she was drinking far less. She also committed to connecting with one family member or friend each day, if only by text or phone. Soon the contacts led to invitations to get together, and Jacquie found herself spending time once again with people she enjoyed.

Eventually, Jacquie was ready to try returning to work. With the support of a rehabilitation counselor and the HR advisor, Jacquie chose to pursue a similar role in a different department, away from the supervisor that she'd found so toxic. Although it seemed clear that he likely wouldn't last much longer in his role, Jacquie didn't want to take the risk of being retraumatized so chose to stay out of his way. Once back at work, Jacquie realized that she was just as competent as she'd ever been and once again started to find her work motivating and meaningful. She had also acquired the resilience to be able to navigate the occasional crisis or setback.

Activities

8.1 Balance Wheel

A balance wheel (a popular model, also known as the wheel of life or balance wheel of life; Clever Memo, n.d.; see Figure 8.1) generally consists of six to eight sections or categories that are deemed important for living a happy, satisfied, and successful life. Depending on the specific model, the sections or categories might change but, in general, would include things like health (i.e., physical, emotional, and spiritual), relationships, work, leisure, and learning.

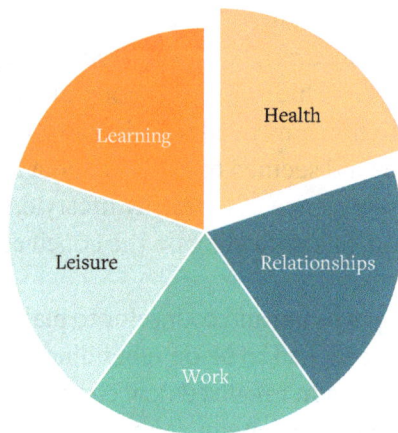

Fig. 8.1 Balance wheel.

As an example, Jacquie considered her wheel from a couple of different perspectives. First, she outlined the categories she deemed most important, and then outlined how she'd like her wheel to look, with relatively even sections indicating how things were well balanced. She recognized, however, that her current wheel didn't at all resemble her ideal one, so this helped her to identify some specific goals for change.

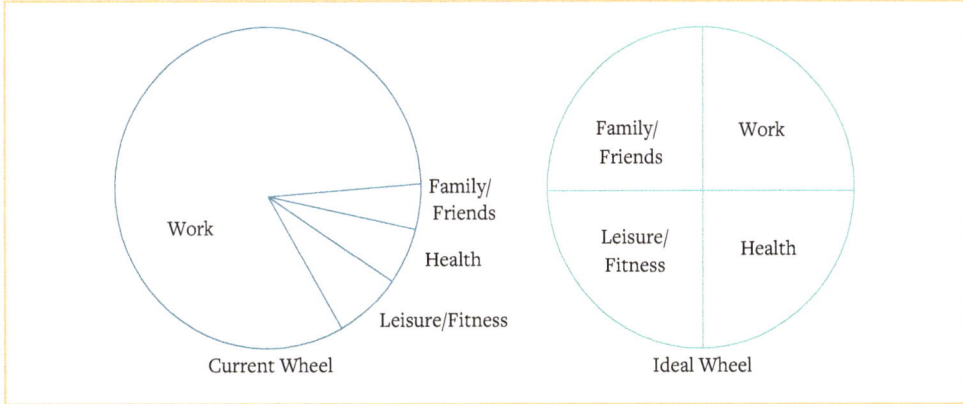

Current Wheel — Work, Family/Friends, Health, Leisure/Fitness

Ideal Wheel — Family/Friends, Work, Leisure/Fitness, Health

Now it's your turn.

Identify the components of your ideal wheel and adjust the sizes of each piece to reflect your priorities if you prefer them to be less balanced. Reflect on what your current wheel looks like. What needs to change to be more aligned with your ideal vision?

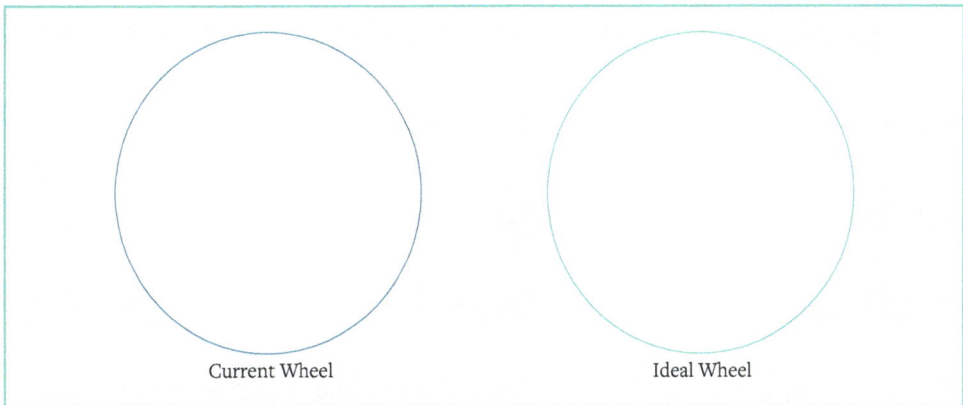

Current Wheel   Ideal Wheel

8.2   What's Working? What's Not?

For each category from your balance wheel, consider both what's working well and what's not working well (adapted from Neault, 2012).

As an example, here's Jacquie's chart.

	What's Working?	What's Not?
Work	I find my work rewarding.	My supervisor
Health		I'm tired and anxious all the time.
Leisure and Fitness		I'm not eating well, and I'm drinking too much. I miss going to the gym.
Family and Friends	My sister has always been supportive.	I haven't been engaging with friends lately.

Now it's your turn.

	What's Working?	What's Not?

What's Working?	What's Not?

Adapted from Roberta Neault, *Career Strategies for a Lifetime of Success*. Copyright © 2012 by Life Strategies Ltd. Reprinted with permission.

8.3   Journaling

Keeping a journal can be an effective way to track activities and experiences as they relate to various parts of the balance wheel and offers an opportunity to reflect on overall well-being. Here is sample from Jacquie's journal.

Date	Activity	Focus	Reflection
06/12/2022	Lunch with sister	Family/friends	It was a bit awkward as she was really worried about me but still nice to reconnect. I don't like feeling fragile.
06/13/2022	Walk around the neighborhood	Health/fitness	I appreciated the fresh air and seeing the local plants and flowers. I didn't really enjoy walking alone, though. I think next time I'll invite my sister along.

Now it's your turn.

Date	Activity	Focus	Reflection
. . . .	. . . .	. . . .	. . . .
. . . .	. . . .	. . . .	. . . .
. . . .	. . . .	. . . .	. . . .
. . . .	. . . .	. . . .	. . . .
. . . .	. . . .	. . . .	. . . .
. . . .	. . . .	. . . .	. . . .
. . . .	. . . .	. . . .	. . . .
. . . .	. . . .	. . . .	. . . .
. . . .	. . . .	. . . .	. . . .
. . . .	. . . .	. . . .	. . . .
. . . .	. . . .	. . . .	. . . .
. . . .	. . . .	. . . .	. . . .
. . . .	. . . .	. . . .	. . . .
. . . .	. . . .	. . . .	. . . .

Date	Activity	Focus	Reflection
....	....	....	....
....	....	....	....
....	....	....	....
....	....	....	....
....	....	....	....
....	....	....	....
....	....	....	....
....	....	....	....

Five Big Ideas

1. **Understand well-being.** There are many physical, emotional, and spiritual factors that contribute to well-being, and the mix is different for each individual, although some of the basics like eating and sleeping well, staying hydrated, and exercising regularly are quite universal.

2. **Identify what's working and what's not, in various life arenas.** Well-being (and lack of it) permeates life roles, so holistic assessment is important.

3. **Realign capacity and challenge.** Optimal engagement occurs when one has sufficient capacity for all of life's current challenges, and vice versa. Too much challenge for capacity is overwhelming. However, underutilized capacity can be discouraging and boring. An excess in either direction can lead to disengagement, which is the opposite of well-being and full engagement in all life arenas.

4. **Build resilience.** Life won't ever be perfect. Being stretched too thin, at work or in any other life roles, doesn't leave energy or space to engage in healthy habits and coping strategies that can mitigate stress. Being proactive instead of reactive can help keep you in the zone of optimal engagement.

5. **Get the help you need.** Seek support from family members, friends, coworkers, supervisors—all of the positive people in your life. When you (or they) are noticing a shift in well-being that seems to be becoming a downward spiral, connect with your family physician or a counselor to help you get back on track.

References

Ariza-Montes, A., Leal-Rodríguez, A. L., Ramírez-Sobrino, J., & Molina-Sánchez, H. (2019). Safeguarding health at the workplace: A study of work engagement, authenticity and subjective wellbeing among religious workers. *International Journal of Environmental Research and Public Health, 16*(17), 3016. https://doi.org/10.3390/ijerph16173016

Bakker, A. B., & Demerouti, E. (2008). Towards a model of work engagement. *Career Development International, 13*, 209–223. https://doi.org/10.1108/13620430810870476

Burns, R. A., Butterworth, P., & Anstey, K. J. (2016). An examination of the long-term impact of job strain on mental health and wellbeing over a 12-year period. *Social Psychiatry and Psychiatric Epidemiology, 51*(5), 725–733. https://doi.org/10.1007/s00127-016-1192-9

Cheng, B. H., & McCarthy, J. M. (2018). Understanding the dark and bright sides of anxiety: A theory of workplace anxiety. *Journal of Applied Psychology, 103*(5), 537–560. https://doi.org/10.1037/apl0000266

Clever Memo. (n.d.). *The balance of life wheel assessment in coaching.* https://clevermemo.com/blog/en/the-balance-of-life-wheel-assessment/

Duxbury, L., & Higgins, C. (2003). *Work-life conflict in Canada in the new millennium: A status report.* Health Canada. https://publications.gc.ca/collections/Collection/H72-21-186-2003E.pdf

Duxbury, L., & Higgins, C. (2009). *Work–life conflict in Canada in the new millennium: Key findings and recommendations from the 2001 national work–life conflict study (Report Six).* Health Canada. http://www.hc-sc.gc.ca/ewh-semt/alt_formats/hecs-sesc/pdf/pubs/occup-travail/balancing_six-equilibre_six/balancing_six-equilibre_six-eng.pdf

Duxbury, L., & Higgins, C. (2012). *Revisiting work-life issues in Canada: The 2012 national study on balancing work and caregiving in Canada.* http://newsroom.carleton.ca/wp-content/files/2012-National-Work-Long-Summary.pdf

Lewis, R., & Donaldson-Feilder, E. (2014). *Managing for sustainable employee engagement.* http://www.mas.org.uk/uploads/artlib/managing-for-sustainable-employee-engagement.pdf

Neault, R. (2012). *Career strategies for a lifetime of success* (3rd ed.). Life Strategies.

Rasool, S. F., Wang, M., Tang, M., Saeed, A., & Iqbal, J. (2021). How toxic workplace environment effects the employee engagement: The mediating role of organizational support and employee wellbeing. *International Journal of Environmental Research and Public Health, 18*(5), 2294. https://doi.org/10.3390/ijerph18052294

Redekopp, D. E., & Huston, M. (2020). *Strengthening mental health through effective career development: A practitioner's guide.* CERIC. https://ceric.ca/publications/strengthening-mental-health-through-effective-career-development-a-practitioners-guide/

Schulte, P. A., Guerin, R. J., Schill, A. L., Bhattacharya, A., Cunningham, T. R., Pandalai, S. P., Eggerth, D., & Stephenson, C. M. (2015). Considerations for incorporating "well-being" in public policy for workers and workplaces. *American Journal of Public Health, 105*(8), e31–e44. https://doi.org/10.2105/AJPH.2015.302616

Figure Credit

CHAPTER NINE

Capacity: Fit

OPENING VIGNETTE

IMG. 9.1

This past year has been a roller coaster of emotions for Kadeesha, with numerous changes and transitions. She celebrated her 40th birthday, her daughter turned 10, she completed her Master of Science in Leadership (with an Organizational Behavior and Development concentration) from Golden Gate University, retired from the U.S. Marine Corps, and finalized her divorce. Next up is a cross-country move, leaving the Virginia/DC area, having spent the last several years at the Human Resources and Organizational Management branch of the Marine Corps, Quantico office, and heading for the sunny skies of California. This move will put her closer to family and to her ex-husband, ensuring they can both play an active role in raising their daughter.

Although Kadeesha feels all these events are positive, she can't help but feel some sense of loss. She was a proud Marine for 20 years, and although she had begun to feel like the Corps was no longer a good fit, letting go was hard. Although she and her husband no longer made sense as a couple, and they remained good friends, ending a marriage was never easy. Starting over in a new state and being closer to family was exciting, but moving was exhausting. As she planned for so many new beginnings, Kadeesha recognized she'd changed a lot over the last several years, personally and professionally. She was committed to finding a workplace that was a good fit for who she was now but that would also have the flexibility to accommodate her ongoing growth and development. She wasn't sure yet whether the new Kadeesha had fully emerged!

With a lot on the go, Kadeesha didn't want to rush into a new work role but also knew she couldn't stay idle for long. She wanted to put her degree to good use and bring her extensive military experience to the private sector.

Exploring the Factor: Fit

The notion of "fit" is well established in both the organizational behavior/development and the vocational guidance literature. In their 2005 meta-analysis, Kristof-Brown et al. identified four key themes: person–job fit, person–organization fit, person–group fit, and person–supervisor fit. They chose to exclude person–vocation fit due to the breadth of research and literature that exists, largely within the domain of career and vocational guidance. Most notably here would be the career-matching theories and frameworks (e.g., Holland's trait factor) that "help people choose careers by systematically comparing personal characteristics to job requirements or workplace roles" (Neault, 2014, p. 131). Although there is some overlap in each of these approaches, "each type of fit considers the relationship between the person and a specific aspect of his/her environment" (Pickerell, 2013, p. 30). Lack of fit in any one of these (e.g., everything fits well, except the relationship with supervisor) can have a negative impact on engagement.

Work and personal values, and the impact these have on job satisfaction and engagement, are also important components of fit. Within vocational guidance, values are seen as important elements to consider within any career planning process (Amundson, 2003; McKinnon & Johnson, 2014; Sharf, 2002), though can, perhaps, be more difficult to measure than other elements (e.g., skills, interests). Although maybe not immediately clear, "value congruence is widely accepted as the defining operationalization of person-organization fit" (Kristof-Brown et al., 2005, p. 285). Value conflicts came up in the vignette for Chapter 8; clearly lack of fit can also impact overall well-being.

Early research into the career engagement model separated work fit (which would connect with both person–job and person–vocation fit) from values alignment. However, in subsequent research, these factors began to cluster more closely, leading to them being combined into simply "fit."

With this in mind, fit had become a key part of Kadeesha's career exploration process as she considered next steps, especially as she recognized how her priorities, values, interests, and skills have changed over time. Although she loved being a Marine and is deeply proud of her years of service, Kadeesha was beginning to see that she needed something different from what the Corps could offer her. Schein's work on career anchors (as cited in Amundson, 2003) is interesting here, as he hypothesized that career anchors take time to evolve, only developing and becoming a factor in career decision-making after one has worked for several years. For Kadeesha, it explains why her life as a Marine does not fit as well as it once did; she recognizes she now needs more autonomy, independence, and creativity than the Corps allows.

Applying Career Engagement

As an African American woman Kadeesha expected to struggle to find role models and mentors in the U.S. Marine Corps. With less than 10% of the Corps being women, the poorest representation of women across all branches of the U.S. military, and even fewer African Americans, she was routinely the only person "like her," but that did not stop her from having a successful career. Even when things seemed overwhelming, Kadeesha was able to find the energy and determination to build her capacity and, in essence, rise to the challenges she was facing. More recently, however, she was finding it tough to see a future for herself, which is why she ultimately retired after she achieved her 20 years of service.

In using the career engagement model to reflect on the past few years, Kadeesha recognized that she was having these huge shifts between feeling overwhelmed and underutilized, rarely settling in the zone of engagement. In considering her experiences of being overwhelmed, Kadeesha admitted she often blamed her work but, in truth, it was simply she had limited capacity to keep up with the demands of work. Completing her graduate work and coming to terms with the end of her marriage was impacting her ability to deal with what, upon reflection, were not unreasonable work demands. If anything, when focusing solely on her work, Kadeesha recognized she was actually underutilized. Kadeesha was a highly skilled and well-educated professional, yet work was no longer motivating or meaningful (i.e., her capacity now exceeded the challenge work presented). This demonstrates the complexity, and impact, of life roles when considering engagement. It was easy for Kadeesha to, in essence, blame her workplace; however, in unpacking career engagement, this was only part of the problem. At work, Kadeesha was underutilized; it was her other life roles causing strain and tension, and consuming all the capacity she had available, that were making everything seem overwhelming. It is through this reflection that Kadeesha could see where she needed intervention to maximize opportunities to stay engaged.

Armed with this knowledge, Kadeesha can begin to explore future opportunities, looking at career engagement overall but also the combined impact that her various life roles may have.

Activities

9.1   Culture Audits

A culture audit can be a great tool for assessing how well someone might fit in an organization. In conducting culture audits, people would ask specific questions or engage in focused research around the characteristics and values of an organization, helping identify "the way things are done," what type of people might be privileged, and how well things align between the public face/mission and what actually occurs in the day-to-day workplace. When assessing corporate culture consider the visible artifacts, any insider language, and common employee traits.

A fulsome culture audit would include researching the company's website, social media, and publications and speaking with employees, often via an informational interview, asking questions like the following:

- What words would you use to describe your organization?
- What is truly important or valued?
- Who gets promoted?
- What gets rewarded?
- What kinds of people fit in best?

As she is just moving to a new city, Kadeesha is in the early stages of her research exploring organizations with offices with a reasonable commute time to where she expects to live. Her preliminary findings exploring one potential employer are shared.

Company Name	Website/Reports	Social Media
ABC Technologies	• CEO's message includes importance of family, education allowances, health plans, and various activities related to charities/community involvement • Images, although probably stock, show broad spectrum of diversity; has a diversity and inclusion customer • Specific mention of hiring program for veterans	• Corporate SM seems to reflect much of what is on website • Very little political commentary • IG stories show employee groups helping with community projects and a softball team • Found Twitter for CEO, VP of finance, and HR director; all seem very consistent with company message, even with "Tweets are my own" comment

Now it's your turn.

Company Name	Website/Reports	Social Media
. . . .	. . . .	. . . .
. . . .	. . . .	. . . .
. . . .	. . . .	. . . .
. . . .	. . . .	. . . .

Company Name	Website/Reports	Social Media
. . . .	. . . .	. . . .
. . . .	. . . .	. . . .
. . . .	. . . .	. . . .
. . . .	. . . .	. . . .

Given what she found during her preliminary research, Kadeesha would really like to learn more and has created list of questions to ask during an informational interview with the HR director.

Company Name	Interviewee	Date
ABC Technologies	HR Director	To be confirmed
What words would you use to describe your organization?		
What is truly important or valued?		
Who gets promoted?		
What gets rewarded?		
What kinds of people fit in best?		

Now it's your turn.

Company Name	Interviewee	Date
. . . .	. . . .	. . . .

What words would you use to describe your organization?

Company Name	Interviewee	Date
. . . .	. . . .	. . . .

What is truly important or valued?

. . . .

. . . .

. . . .

. . . .

. . . .

Who gets promoted?

. . . .

. . . .

. . . .

. . . .

. . . .

What gets rewarded?

. . . .

. . . .

. . . .

. . . .

. . . .

What kinds of people fit in best?

. . . .

. . . .

. . . .

. . . .

. . . .

9.2 Values Checklist

In starting over, Kadeesha really wants to make sure her values are aligned to her new employer and industry. To begin, she completed a values checklist, selecting values that she felt were important, even very important, in this next stage of her career.

Aesthetics	Independence	People
☐ Appreciating beauty	☒ Autonomy	☐ Altruism
Belonging	☒ Lifestyle freedom	☐ Community involvement
☐ Caring supervisor	☒ Minimal supervision	☐ Cultural identity
☐ Family atmosphere	☒ Time flexibility	☐ Helping others
☐ Friendly coworkers	☐ Working alone	☐ Helping society
☐ Social relations	**Knowledge**	☐ Moral fulfillment
Challenge	☐ Ability utilization	☐ Public contact
☐ Advancement	☐ Being an expert	☐ Social interaction
☐ Adventure	☐ Intellectual stimulation	☐ Time for family
☐ Change and variety	☒ Interesting work	☐ Working with others
Competition	**Leadership**	**Publicity**
☐ Excitement	☐ Authority	☐ Recognition
☐ Fast pace	☐ Influencing people	☐ Status
☐ Physical activity	☐ Making decisions	**Quality**
☐ Physical challenge	☐ Management	☐ Achieving results
☐ Risk	☐ Power	☐ Precision work
☐ Travel	☐ Supervision	**Stability**
☐ Work under pressure	**Money**	☐ Routine
Creativity	☐ High pay/rewards	☐ Safe, good conditions
☐ Artistic creativity	☐ Steady income	☐ Scheduled work
☐ Problem-solving		☐ Secure, regular pay
☐ Program development		
☐ Self-expression		

Now it's your turn.

Aesthetics	Independence	People
☐ Appreciating beauty	☐ Autonomy	☐ Altruism
Belonging	☐ Lifestyle freedom	☐ Community involvement
☐ Caring supervisor	☐ Minimal supervision	☐ Cultural identity
☐ Family atmosphere	☐ Time flexibility	☐ Helping others
☐ Friendly coworkers	☐ Working alone	☐ Helping society
☐ Social relations	**Knowledge**	☐ Moral fulfillment
Challenge	☐ Ability utilization	☐ Public contact
☐ Advancement	☐ Being an expert	☐ Social interaction
☐ Adventure	☐ Intellectual stimulation	☐ Time for family
☐ Change and variety	☐ Interesting work	☐ Working with others
Competition	**Leadership**	**Publicity**
☐ Excitement	☐ Authority	☐ Recognition
☐ Fast pace	☐ Influencing people	☐ Status
☐ Physical activity	☐ Making decisions	**Quality**
☐ Physical challenge	☐ Management	☐ Achieving results
☐ Risk	☐ Power	☐ Precision work
☐ Travel	☐ Supervision	**Stability**
☐ Work under pressure	**Money**	☐ Routine
Creativity	☐ High pay/rewards	☐ Safe, good conditions
☐ Artistic creativity	☐ Steady income	☐ Scheduled work
☐ Problem solving		☐ Secure, regular pay
☐ Program development		
☐ Self-expression		

Five Big Ideas

1. **Fit can take many forms.** Remember that fit can relate to the specific work role, in a specific industry or for a specific employer; it can also relate to colleagues/teammates and even supervisors and to characteristics and values. Be sure to reflect on the specific areas where a lack of fit may be impacting engagement and target interventions/activities accordingly.

2. **Be willing to shift.** Fit, or lack thereof, can sometimes be out of your control, possibly leaving some type of shift as the only option available. If the occupational role, industry, and colleagues are a great fit but your supervisor is making work unbearable there may be little you can do, other than considering a shift to a new department or even workplace.

3. **Consider your priorities.** Rarely in life do we find the perfect fit—in clothing, houses, or work. When considering what may need to shift, identify your priorities, and consider where the pain is greatest. Sometimes multiple shifts need to happen over time rather than finding the perfect fit with a single move.

4. **Recognize how things have changed.** How you fit, and your motivations or reasons for working, are likely to change over time. Acknowledge how life and work experiences have impacted who you are as a unique individual and perhaps even changed your priorities. Don't see these changes as problems to be solved but, rather, as natural growth.

5. **Explore how fit is impacting career engagement.** Remember that directionality is a core component of career engagement. When considering fit, or lack thereof, explore whether this is resulting in you feeling more underutilized or overwhelmed.

References

Amundson, N. E. (2003). *Active engagement* (2nd ed.). Ergon Communications.

Kristof-Brown, A. L., Zimmerman, R. D., & Johnson, E. C. (2005). Consequences of individuals' fit at work: A meta-analysis of person-job, person-organization, person-group, and person-supervisor fit. *Personnel Psychology, 58*(2), 281–342. http://dx.doi.org/10.1111%2Fj.1744-6570.2005.00672.x

McKinnon, K., & Johnson, K. (2014). Career planning, knowledge, and skills. In B. C. Shepard, & P. S. Mani (Eds.), *Career development practice in Canada: Perspectives, principles, and professionalism* (pp. 173–198). CERIC.

Neault, R. A. (2014). Theoretical foundations of career development. In B. C. Shepard, & P. S. Mani (Eds.), *Career development practice in Canada: Perspectives, principles, and professionalism* (pp. 129–152). CERIC.

Pickerell, D. A. (2013). *Examining the career engagement of Canadian career development practitioners* [Unpublished doctoral dissertation]. Fielding Graduate University.

Sharf, R. S. (2002). *Applying career development theory to counseling.* Brooks/Cole.

Figure Credit

PART II

Working With Career Engagement

CHAPTER TEN

Career Engagement for Individuals

OPENING VIGNETTE

IMG. 10.1

Sonya had worked for a high-end, family-owned furniture company for the past 6 years. Soon after starting there, she'd been in a car accident, resulting in some permanent disabilities to her legs and back. The company had been amazingly supportive during her recovery, shifting her from sales to IT services so that she could work in the office at a desk rather than make off-site sales calls or spend all day on her feet during shifts in the product showroom. Although her mobility had improved a bit over the years, from requiring a wheelchair for the first 6 months back at work to eventually being able to manage with a cane, Sonya had struggled with chronic pain and was always exhausted by the end of her workday. That changed during the COVID-19 pandemic, when the office shut down and everyone was required to work from home for 18 months.

Sonya found that not having a commute to work had made all the difference in the world to her stamina and pain management. In the first few months, she began to have energy to do more things around her house again. For the first time in years, she began baking and had gradually stocked her freezer with muffins, cookies, and healthy home-cooked meals. She appreciated being able to integrate her household chores with her workday, rather than filling her weekends with everything that needed to be done at home. Working from home, Sonya was better able to rest when she needed to—even lying down during some Zoom meetings when she didn't need to have her camera on. As her manager started talking about return-to-work planning, Sonya was reminded of the early months after her accident. She remembered how hard it had been to go into the office each day. Now that she knew she could do her job effectively from home, returning to the daily commute and trying to fit all her chores and errands into the weekend felt exhausting and overwhelming.

Exploring Career Engagement for Individuals

The career engagement model, with all its components, was introduced in earlier chapters of this book. In essence, optimal engagement, at work and in other life roles, is achieved through a careful alignment of challenge and capacity. As previously described, challenge consists of both motivating work and meaningful opportunities. Capacity, on the other hand, comprises many factors, including resources, relationships, workload, well-being, and fit. Other researchers have identified the importance of social support and positive emotions to higher levels of career engagement (Hirschi & Freund, 2012), as well as the impact of attending to employees' unique career needs and motivators in enhancing both their engagement and job commitment (Coetzee et al., 2014). It is widely understood that engaged workers are less likely to leave and are more productive, contributing positively overall to an organization's bottom line (Stange, 2020). Attending to career engagement can be particularly important during times of significant career transitions (Pickerell, 2017); the post-COVID return-to-work planning that was the backdrop of Sonya's story in the opening vignette is a good example of a significant transition, even though Sonya would like to keep the same job. At this pivotal time, it might be helpful for Sonya and her manager to engage in job crafting to ensure that she's able to maintain the relatively pain-free condition that she had achieved from working at home during the first several months of the pandemic; job crafting has been positively linked to engagement (Brucker & Sundar, 2020).

Applying Career Engagement

In this chapter's vignette, Sonya has finally been able to achieve optimal engagement, 6 years into her recovery from a debilitating car accident. She likes how it feels and is overwhelmed at the thought of losing it if she needs to return to the office again, with the exhausting daily commute. Sonya reflected on what had been different over the past year and a half while working from home. She realized that she thoroughly enjoyed the day-to-day challenges of her work—they were both meaningful and motivating. She appreciated her team and how they'd managed to stay connected and have fun together, even when only meeting through Zoom. Her manager was amazing. Always respectful, kind, and compassionate, but also able to pull the very best from the team. Together they'd developed innovative and cost-saving solutions for the company and had contributed to positive growth during a time when other similar organizations were losing money or, in some cases, even shutting down.

Despite how wonderful work was, Sonya also remembered how tired she used to be at the end of each workday. It was painful getting to and from the car or bus each day; it wasn't the length of the commute, but it was the transition from work or home to her transportation that was hard. Even within the office, getting from her desk to conference rooms or joining others for coffee or lunch in the staffroom or nearby restaurants was painful, exhausting, and time-consuming. Weekends, instead of providing time for rest, had been consumed with household chores and errands.

Thinking about the plans for returning to work in the office, Sonya realized how different and relatively pain free her life had become while working from home. She didn't want to risk losing her job and certainly didn't want her team members to see her as less competent than them or getting any special privileges. However, she also recognized that she was better able to bring her "best self" to work when she was working from home. She began to make a plan to talk to her manager about the possibility of continuing to work from home, perhaps even just for 3–4 days each week.

Activities

There are several things you can strategically do on your own to achieve and maintain optimal engagement, at work and in your other life roles. Sonya's reflections illustrate how walking through this process can help with making a plan to optimize engagement.

10.1   Monitor Your Career Engagement

Use the career engagement model to identify your current engagement level: disengaged (overwhelmed), overwhelmed, engaged, underutilized, or disengaged (underutilized). Mark an "X" below where you see your fit. Set yourself tasks to reassess at regular intervals (e.g., 3, 6, 9, and 12 months). Make any relevant notes regarding your career, life, and/or learning context that might impact your engagement levels.

Here is a sample from Sonya.

Date	D(O)	O	E	U	D(U)	Notes
03/04/2022			X			Wow, almost pain free and not exhausted. Working from home makes such a difference.
12/06/2022	X					Supervisor advised they're looking at us returning to the office.

Now it's your turn.

Date	D(O)	O	E	U	D(U)	Notes
						....
						....
						....

Date	D(O)	O	E	U	D(U)	Notes
						....
						....
						....
						....
						....
						....
						....
						....
						....
						....
						....
						....

10.2   What's Working? What's Not?

Identify three to four life roles (e.g., work, student, parent/child, community member). For each, life role consider what's working well and not so well.

Here is a sample from Sonya.

Life Role	What's Working	What's Not?
Employee	Working from home is great for my overall health. I feel I can contribute in more meaningful ways. Our team still manages to have fun, troubleshoot issues, and be innovative.	I'm worried I'll feel disconnected if I stay online and coworkers return to the office.
Homemaker	I feel like I have so much more time for errands and also just having "me time."	

Now it's your turn.

Life Role	What's Working	What's Not?
....	....	....
....	....	....
....	....	....
....	....	....
....	....	....
....	....	....
....	....	....
....	....	....
....	....	....
....	....	....
....	....	....
....	....	....
....	....	....
....	....	....
....	....	....
....	....	....
....	....	....
....	....	....
....	....	....
....	....	....
....	....	....

10.3   Know Yourself

Reflect on your personal attributes and record them in the table provided. Refer to assessment reports if applicable.

Here is a sample from Sonya.

Motivated Skills	Interests	Values	Personal Style
Technology Critical thinking Sales	Baking	Teamwork Flexibility	

Now it's your turn.

Motivated Skills	Interests	Values	Personal Style
....	....	....	....
....	....	....	....
....	....	....	....
....	....	....	....
....	....	....	....

10.4   Explore Opportunities

Reflect on opportunities within all areas of your life.

Here is a sample from Sonya.

At Home	At School	At Work	In the Community
Integrating household chores and activities within my workday has left evenings and weekends open for other activities I enjoy (e.g., baking)	May be a good time to take some additional IT certifications now that I feel I have more energy and time	Arrange a flexible work arrangement where I only have to commute into the office a few times	Get involved in community activities, maybe selling my baked goods at the local farm market on the weekend

Now it's your turn.

At Home	At School	At Work	In the Community
. . . .	. . . .	. . . .	. . . .
. . . .	. . . .	. . . .	. . . .
. . . .	. . . .	. . . .	. . . .
. . . .	. . . .	. . . .	. . . .

10.5   Identify a Starting Point

Identify a reasonable change you can make at this time to improve or maintain your level of engagement. This can be a small or big shift; choose something reasonable for your current context—something you have both individual capacity for and external resources to support.

Here is a sample from Sonya.

Change	Individual Characteristics	External Resources
Return to the office no more than once a week, as needed	I'm excited to see my team in person I'm feeling more rested	My team knows that work can be done remotely My supervisor is supportive and understanding

Now it's your turn.

Change	Individual Characteristics	External Resources
. . . .	. . . .	. . . .
. . . .	. . . .	. . . .
. . . .	. . . .	. . . .
. . . .	. . . .	. . . .

Next, set a specific short-term and long-term SMART goal related to the change you'd like to make.

Here is a sample from Sonya.

		Is your goal ...				
		Specific	Measurable	Achievable	Relevant	Time-Limited
Short-term	Support a pain-free, balanced lifestyle by arranging a flexible work arrangement (limited to 1 or less days on site per week) with current supervisor by July 1st.	☒	☒	☒	☒	☒
Long-term	Reengage with my local community by selling my baked goods at the local farm market on weekends within 3 years.	☒	☒	☒	☒	☒

Now it's your turn.

		Is your goal ...				
		Specific	Measurable	Achievable	Relevant	Time-Limited
Short-term	....	☐	☐	☐	☐	☐
Long-term	....	☐	☐	☐	☐	☐

10.6   Avoid Disengagement

Reflect on moments where you've felt overwhelmed or underutilized. Record your early warning signs and brainstorm strategies you could implement to mitigate the risk of disengagement.

Here is a sample from Sonya.

Early Warning Signs	Strategies
My email inbox has over 10 urgently flagged items	Prioritizing urgent items with a supervisor or co-worker
I need to take more than three pain breaks during workday	Proactively scheduling more regular breaks throughout the workday

Now it's your turn.

Early Warning Signs	Strategies

Five Big Ideas

1. **Take a holistic approach.** Know yourself (i.e., interests, values, personal style, and skills) and consider all life roles (i.e., parent, spouse, volunteer) when assessing your engagement.

2. **Decide on how much to shift.** Building from your reflections, identify a reasonable shift you can make at this time to improve or maintain your level of engagement.

3. **Take on an appropriate level of challenge**. Reflect on what level of challenge would be appropriate relative to your current capacity. What could you take on? What could you give up?

4. **Set short- and long-term goals.** Identify goals to help improve or maintain your level of engagement. Ensure goals are specific, measurable, achievable, relevant, and time limited.

5. **Avoid disengagement.** Learn from moments when you've felt overwhelmed or underutilized. What early-warning signs can signal issues ahead? Brainstorm strategies to implement that can mitigate the risk of disengagement.

References

Brucker, D. L., & Sundar, V. (2020). Job crafting among American workers with disabilities. *Journal of Occupational Rehabilitation, 30,* 575–587. https://doi.org/10.1007/s10926-020-09889-9

Coetzee, M., Schreuder, D., & Tladinyane, R. (2014). Employees' work engagement and job commitment: The moderating role of career anchors. *SA Journal of Human Resource Management, 12*(1). https://doi.org/10.4102/sajhrm.v12i1.572

Hirschi, A., & Freund, P. A. (2014). Career engagement: Investigating intraindividual predictors of weekly fluctuations in proactive career behaviors. *Career Development Quarterly, 62,* 5–20. https://doi.org/10.1002/j.2161-0045.2014.00066.x

Pickerell, D. (2017). Staying engaged during times of transition. *CEAV, 44*(3), 21. https://ceav.vic.edu.au/media/173805/ceav_ejournal_edition3_17_web_final.pdf

Stange, J. (2020, September 24). *How to improve employee engagement.* Quantum Workplace. https://www.quantumworkplace.com/future-of-work/how-to-improve-employee-engagement

Figure Credit

CHAPTER ELEVEN

Career Engagement for Managers, Supervisors, and Coaches

OPENING VIGNETTE

IMG. 11.1

Marcel is the manager of IT Services for a high-end, family-owned furniture company. His small team includes web designers, network and hardware technicians, IT security specialists, and general software support personnel. The team supports a few physical locations, including a small head office, a larger warehouse located within about a 15-minute walk, as well as three boutique stores strategically located throughout the larger regional district. The IT team has dedicated workspace in the head office and the warehouse and, although they could all work in one location, it was more common for the team to distribute themselves across the two key locations, ensuring someone was available to support on-site staff. Visits to the stores were rare, as any IT-related problems could generally be solved via remote access. That was until the COVID-19 pandemic forced the closure of the three stores, head office, and much of the warehouse, resulting in most staff working remotely as they pivoted to fully online sales.

Now that reopening is on the horizon, Marcel is exploring options for flexible work and is discovering his team has a lot of opinions about their anticipated return to working on-site. As they've demonstrated throughout the pandemic, technically all the team can work remotely, only physically going to one of the two locations when required. Based on a quick anonymous survey, Marcel learned that some members of his team would prefer to continue with full remote work, whereas others would prefer a hybrid model. There are, however, external pressures to consider as the store owners seem to prefer everyone on-site and, of course, any staff in the stores must be onsite full-time. As such, Marcel is trying to balance his team's preferences with the evolving expectations of company leadership. All of this is further complicated by changing public health orders that must continue to respond to COVID transmission rates and vaccination data throughout the community.

Adding to this complexity are Marcel's own preferences, coupled with how to best support Sonya, a member of his team, introduced in the Chapter 10 vignette, who was seriously injured in a car accident several years ago. Sonya continues to struggle with chronic pain as a result of the accident and was showing signs of exhaustion and burnout prior to the COVID-19 shutdown. Marcel has been working with Sonya and the human resources team to figure out how to best accommodate her. As Sonya clearly prefers working from home full-time, and it seems better for her health, that challenge still looms.

Exploring Career Engagement for Managers, Supervisors, and Coaches

As outlined in the previous chapters, career engagement is realized through the dynamic interaction of challenge and capacity and, within each of these components, exist several factors that impact opportunities to maximize engagement. Although many of these factors may seem more individually focused, organizational influences must not be overlooked.

A plethora of engagement literature and research outlines the important role managers and supervisors have in creating an engaged workforce (Anitha, 2014; Barik & Kochar, 2017; Ladyshewsky & Taplin, 2018; Lee et al., 2017; Thompson, n.d.). There can, of course, be some notable differences depending on how engagement is being perceived (i.e., work, job, employee) and other factors that would also support engagement. For example, a supportive manager/supervisor will likely have minimal impact on engagement if the overall organizational culture is toxic or if coworkers are hostile.

Ladyshewsky and Taplin (2018) noted that "there is significant evidence of a positive relationship between manager as coach and work engagement" (p. 14), but again this can be mitigated by the organizational culture. Similarly, Jin and McDonald (2016) found that an "expression of caring and concern by a supervisor can create a sense of obligation on the part of employees to reciprocate with greater levels of work engagement" (p. 16).

In his book *Seeing Systems*, Barry Oshry (2007) looked at organizations as systems, simplifying, to some degree, a structure of tops (executives), middles (managers), and bottoms (workers), noting that "if we are paying attention, we know what life is like for us in our part of the system. Other parts of the system are, for the most part invisible to us" (p. 1). Managers and supervisors, therefore, are often in between with pressure coming down from the top, but not always all the information needed, combined with pressure coming up from the bottom but perhaps with limited understanding of the day-to-day experiences. The same challenges would exist with managers who are seeking to improve engagement; as their context/view shifts, so too might their interventions.

In a similar vein, Patton and McMahon's (2006) systems theory framework of career development (STF) also provides important context in exploring the manager's role in supporting engagement. Within STF, the "individual system [and] the contextual system, including the social system and the environmental-societal system" (p. 197) are important reminders to managers that the individual workers, and their teams, are subject to internal and external influences that could impact opportunities for engagement. Many of these would comprise the capacity component of the career engagement model, but, from a systems perspective, it would be important to consider the individual, the organization, and the broader environment.

Applying Career Engagement

The past year and a half has been an interesting time for Marcel and his team. When the pandemic forced a massive lockdown, company leadership had no choice but to scale back operations, including closing the three stores and shifting to a fully online storefront. The company did all they could to keep everyone working, even the salespeople who often had very little to do. There was a lot of turmoil and chaos throughout the organization, though Marcel's team wasn't impacted as much as other employees. IT shifted to remote work relatively seamlessly, but as Marcel reflects, many were likely overwhelmed trying to set up their own workspaces while concurrently helping other employees transition to remote work.

The team quickly settled into a routine, for work and connections. Marcel knew his team was close-knit, often going for coffee and lunch together. He really tried to encourage a culture of open communication, support, and fun, believing that an important component of his job was to ensure his team had all they needed to bring their best selves to work. Early into the closure, Marcel scheduled weekly "coffee" breaks that had every member of the team join a video call just to share how things were going and talk about shows they were binge watching or books they were reading. Some weeks they even played games, including Scrabble and Name That Tune. Marcel also booked time with the various sub-teams to ensure there was ongoing communication around updates, challenges, and needs and to give him an opportunity to inform the team of any corporate communications he could share.

Marcel did his best to gain a good understanding of how individual staff were doing and was, at times, surprised at the various reports he received. Some weren't doing as well as he would have expected; others were thriving in the remote environment, even within a lockdown. Sonya (introduced in Chapter 10) was a great example. The transition to IT after her car accident hadn't been an easy one; the new team and specialized skills and knowledge required often overwhelmed her in the beginning, especially as she was dealing with so much in her personal life. In hindsight though, it hadn't taken long for Sonya to really thrive in her new role, and she was a great fit for the team Marcel had very carefully built. Team dynamics was something Marcel paid close attention to as a manager; yes, he needed people who had a specific set of skills and knowledge, but, more importantly, he needed people who could work effectively together.

Marcel prided himself on giving his team the space they needed to be successful and engaged in their work roles, while always being available should someone begin to feel overwhelmed or underutilized. This is where the influence of Vygotsky's (1978) zone of proximal development can be seen in the career engagement model. Marcel understood that his team had complex work and personal lives, sometimes resulting in shifts in and out of the zone of engagement, or within the zone. Marcel's role was to provide some scaffolding around the pieces he could control, doing his best to ensure that the work remained motivating and meaningful, that the team had an appropriate amount of work and access to needed resources, and that the individual and environmental influences that impacted each of his team members, and the team as a collective, were acknowledged and accommodated. Marcel also recognized that although some elements were within his control, there were numerous other factors that he couldn't even influence. In return-to-work discussions, Marcel worked hard to balance the needs and preferences of the individual members of his team, recognizing how these had the potential to impact team dynamics while also considering the expectations of leadership and other employees.

All the while, Marcel had to remain aware of his own career engagement. He was very wise to recognize that if his engagement was suffering it would have a devastating impact on his team.

Activities

11.1   Motivating Projects and Meaningful Opportunities

Providing motivating projects and activities, as well as meaningful opportunities, will help you as a manager, supervisor, or coach to foster an environment conducive to optimal career engagement. Reflect on what your team finds motivating and meaningful. You can assess this through informal conversation or via more formal methods such as a team-wide survey.

Marcel began this activity by looking at his team, as a collective unit, carefully noting any individual differences he was aware of.

What motivates my team?	Pride in their work and a sense of accomplishment Being a trusted source of knowledge and expertise
What projects might incorporate these motivators?	IT retrofit in the warehouse Integration of new online store site into existing website Consideration of a new POS system
What is meaningful for my team?	
What projects might be more appealing?	

Now it's your turn.

What motivates my team?

....

....

....

....

What projects might incorporate these motivators?

....

....

....

....

What is meaningful for my team?

....

....

....

....

What projects might be more appealing?

....

....

....

....

11.2   Key Influencers

In any work team, there are going to be some key influencers that support the career engagement of others. Sometimes these are managers/supervisors/team leaders, but they may simply be members of the team that others gravitate to or confide in. Identify the key influencers and record what tools/resources they'd need to support engagement efforts.

Marcel did this for his team, identifying a couple of key influencers.

Key Influencer	Tools/Resources Required
Sonya	100% remote work Flexible hours
Pravneet	Opportunity to offer/design regular training; she loves teaching others and creating content
Castor	Upgraded/larger monitor

Now it's your turn.

Key Influencer	Tools/Resources Required

11.3 Provide Relevant Resources

Record what resources your group already has access to and what resources they still require, now and perhaps in future. Remember that, as outlined in Chapter 5, resources can include people and time.

Marcel's reflections are provided.

What You Have	What You Need
A strong team with good communication	Plan for in-person meetings/get-togethers that include everyone, with sufficient notice for Sonya to adjust as it is important that she is included
Appropriate equipment, though perhaps some items need to be adjusted	Jaskaran will need a new laptop and company cell phone
Technical skill and know-how	Improved project/task planning to support hybrid workforce

Now it's your turn.

What You Have	What You Need

What You Have	What You Need
....	....
....	....
....	....
....	....
....	....
....	....
....	....
....	....
....	....
....	....
....	....
....	....

11.4   Strengthen Relationships

Identify a peer relationship challenge you anticipate in your group and record a strategy to address it.

Marcel's reflections helped him to identify some immediate action steps to take.

Peer Relationship Challenge	Strategy to Address
Sonya and Pravneet are struggling to get along, yet had always worked well together	Meet with each 1:1 to try to get a sense of what happened, then work toward a solution. Ultimately, they are on different teams, so only a huge problem if this starts to impact others
The whole team, me included, with the sales staff. Seems to stem from resentment related to working remotely	Meet with Rebecca, HR director, to discuss concerns and perhaps facilitate a discussion with Marcel and Thomas, the sales manager

Now it's your turn.

Peer Relationship Challenge	Strategy to Address

11.5   Critically Assess Workload

Identify current and anticipated projects that you will need to monitor.

Marcel found this helpful in identifying a few potential risks and how to mitigate them.

The IT retrofit in the warehouse is going to be a huge project, consuming a lot of resources. At this time we should be okay, unless another location runs into any problems. Make note to connect with external contractor used in the past to discuss their availability to act as backup.

Integration of new online store site into existing website should be easy, but concerns RE: Sonya and Pravneet's relationship could impact this project.

Consideration of a new POS system; Castor will need to source possible vendors, review proposals, and make recommendations.

Now it's your turn.

Identify current and anticipated projects that you will need to monitor.

> ....
>
> ....
>
> ....
>
> ....

11.6   Facilitate Health and Wellness

In the table provided, record any concerns you may have, what resources your group already has access to, and what they may require in future.

In reflecting on this, Marcel identified some important next steps.

Health and Wellness Concerns	Current Resources	Needed Resources
Sonya	Seems to have all she needs in her home-based office	None at the moment, but her staying 100% remote is still being sorted out
Stress, anxiety: everyone	Self-help pamphlets	The whole organization, not just our team, needs some in-service related to managing health and wellness, especially related to the stress and anxiety that everyone has experienced over the past several months as well as coping post-lockdown
COVID vaccines	Marcel wasn't sure where this fit, but he does know that the company is not mandating vaccines and also not asking employees to disclose. Although Marcel truly understands, this is creating a challenge in planning a return to work. Some members of his team, for example, would be more in favor of more time on-site if they felt confident their exposure risk was minimal	

Now it's your turn.

Health and Wellness Concerns	Current Resources	Needed Resources

11.7   Recognize the Importance of Fit

Use the table provided to identify key areas (e.g., degrees, credentials, values) where individuals in your group may vary and record how this may impact fit.

Through this activity, Marcel recognized some key differences that could impact his team going forward.

Area	Impact on Fit
Autonomy and independence	Things vary a little bit here, with some individuals preferring autonomy and others wanting to return to the days we could congregate in the lunchroom. This continues to be a work in progress and something that must be monitored closely
Credentials	Team is highly educated, specific to their various areas of focus. May explore some soft-skill credentials related to having effective conversations or emotional intelligence
Helping others	Some differences here as well, with some members a bit more committed to our role as a service unit, geared at helping other teams with their technologies, versus some measure of staff understanding how to use their tech effectively.

Now it's your turn.

Area	Impact on Fit
. . . .	. . . .
. . . .	. . . .
. . . .	. . . .
. . . .	. . . .
. . . .	. . . .
. . . .	. . . .
. . . .	. . . .
. . . .	. . . .
. . . .	. . . .
. . . .	. . . .
. . . .	. . . .
. . . .	. . . .
. . . .	. . . .
. . . .	. . . .
. . . .	. . . .
. . . .	. . . .

11.8   Align Challenge and Capacity

Brainstorm what contributes to the level of challenge for your group, as well as capacity (internal/external).

Marcel was able to identify some mismatches and opportunities for building capacity.

Challenge	Capacity
IT is always changing; computers always present a challenge	Team is well trained, and some budget money has been released for some online courses, which will help the team stay up to speed on new technologies
Some non-IT staff don't have the technical skills they really need; even managing email seems tough for some people	Pravneet is really interested in staff training; perhaps she could design some micro modules to help fill skills gaps. In turn, this may reduce tech support calls

Next, identify strategies you will implement to maintain the alignment of challenge and capacity in your group.

Marcel's reflections helped him to recognize some important considerations.

Perhaps not a strategy but something I'll monitor is watching for the subtle signs such as team members who aren't contributing as much as they used to or who have dropped hints that things aren't going well. The pandemic lasted for so long that, even though people may have adjusted to working from home quite well, a return to the office—even part-time—is another change and adjustment.

Now it's your turn.

Challenge	Capacity

Identify strategies you will implement to maintain the alignment of challenge and capacity in your group.

_____

Five Big Ideas

1. **Monitor the dynamic interaction of challenge and capacity, watching for signs of disengagement.** The natural ebbs and flows to work, and life, will impact people's experiences of engagement. Watch for the subtle signs of movement toward being overwhelmed or underutilized and act accordingly. Pay attention to when disengagement may be on the horizon; early recognition and intervention can mitigate bigger problems.

2. **Recognize the importance of fit.** When adding to your team, think beyond skills and knowledge, and focus on traits, characteristics, and shared values. These can be harder to assess, but without considering fit from this perspective, it may cause turmoil at some point. At the same time, avoid hiring more of the same, which can often exacerbate blind spots.

3. **Be mindful of other life roles.** It really isn't feasible for employees to leave their personal lives at the door. Recognize that life happens. Kids get sick, marriages begin and end, and loved ones die; people go to school and engage in activities outside of work. The demands of other life roles can, through no one's fault, impact the capacity available for work. Even when there is little that managers can do, being supportive and understanding is an important first step.

4. **Optimize a healthy workplace culture.** Managers and supervisors are just as responsible as HR for ensuring a healthy workplace culture, perhaps even more so. Recommend and support initiatives geared at promoting a mentally and physically healthy workplace. Praise employees who choose to stay home rather than coming to work sick, create safe and inclusive spaces where employees can share

success and express concerns, and lead by example, ensuring your commitment isn't just corporate speak but something you truly value.

5. **Don't neglect your own career engagement.** It only makes sense that a disengaged manager/supervisor will be largely unable to support the engagement of others. Take time to assess whether your work role remains a good fit, offering meaningful and motivating opportunities, providing sufficient resources, and nurturing supportive relationships.

References

Anitha, J. (2014). Determinants of employee engagement and their impact on employee performance. *International Journal of Productivity and Performance Management, 63*(3), 308–323. https://doi.org/10.1108/IJPPM-01-2013-0008

Barik, S., & Kochar, A. (2017). Antecedents and consequences of employee engagement: A literature review. *International Journal of Latest Technology in Engineering, Management & Applied Science, 6*(4), 33–38. https://www.ijltemas.in/DigitalLibrary/Vol.6Issue4/33-38.pdf

Jin, M. H., & McDonald, B. (2016). Understanding employee engagement in the public sector: The role of immediate supervisor, perceived organizational support, and learning opportunities. *The American Review of Public Administration, 47*(8), 1–23. https://doi.org/10.1177/0275074016643817

Ladyshewsky, R. K., & Taplin, R. (2018). The interplay between organisational learning culture, the manager as coach, self-efficacy and workload on employee work engagement. *International Journal of Evidence Based Coaching and Mentoring, 16*(2), 3–19. https://doi.org/10.24384/000483

Lee, M. C. C., Idris, M. A., & Delfabbro, P. H. (2017). The linkages between hierarchical culture and empowering leadership and their effects on employees' work engagement: Work meaningfulness as a mediator. *International Journal of Stress Management, 24*(4), 392–415. https://doi.org/10.1037/str0000043

Oshry, B. (2007). *Seeing systems: Unlocking the mysteries of organization life* (2nd ed.). Berrett-Koehler.

Patton, W., & McMahon, M. (2006). *Career development and systems theory: Connecting theory and practice* (2nd ed.). Sense.

Thompson, C. (n.d.). *The manager jackpot: Simple HR solutions for building better bosses*. Quantum Workplace.

Vygotsky, L. S. (1978). *Mind and society: The development of higher psychological processes* (M. Cole, V. John-Steiner, S. Scribner, & E. Souberman, Eds.). Harvard University Press. https://doi.org/10.2307/j.ctvjf9vz4

Figure Credit

CHAPTER TWELVE

Career Engagement for Leaders and Policymakers

OPENING VIGNETTE

IMG. 12.1

It had been a challenging 18 months for Misha. As head of human resources for her family's high-end furniture store, the COVID-19 pandemic resulted in a lot of changes for her, her family, and their employees. They had survived though, despite lockdowns, supply chain issues, and even a personal COVID experience that almost killed her Babička, "Babi" as everyone called her.

Perhaps the silver lining was that her grandfather was finally letting go, leaving the operation of their family business to her father, her two brothers, and herself. Her grandfather was an incredible man, from very humble beginnings as a craftsman—and a maker of the most beautiful wood furniture—to the head of a very successful set of stores, known for unique, specialty pieces. At one time, he'd traveled the world seeking artisans whose work could be featured in their stores.

Misha's father Kael, and brother Kael Jr., rivaled her grandfather in their woodworking skills, though only her brother worked with wood anymore. For many years, her father had taken over as chief operating officer, basically running the company—as much as grandfather would allow, anyway. Her father loved his role, but she also knew he sometimes missed the hours spent working with wood and was envious of his youngest son who spent a lot of time in the shop. Too much time if you asked Misha as Kael Jr. had craftspeople all over the world and a supply chain to manage. Radek, the eldest brother and current VP of marketing and sales, and Misha worked closely with their father, at the head office. Collectively, they were proud of their family's legacy. Their employees didn't seem overly impacted by the most recent adjustments in senior leadership; any of the employees from her "grandfather's day" had long since retired and, although there were some workers who pre-dated Misha and her brother's arrival, they'd grown up in and around the business, so weren't unfamiliar faces.

With the worst of the COVID pandemic fading into memory, the family, and some of their senior team, are planning their reopening. A key sticking point seems to be which workers need to be back to the office and warehouse, who can shift to hybrid, and who can work fully, or mostly, remotely. Employees are like family, and the environment, across all their locations, was professional and respectful, as any business would be, but was also full of laughter and many positive relationships that often spilled over into their personal lives. While Misha and her brothers felt this was an opportunity to really hear what their employees were asking for, Misha's dad, albeit with some pressure from her grandfather, was demanding everyone come back to work.

Exploring Career Engagement for Leaders and Policymakers

As noted throughout the previous chapters, career engagement doesn't occur in a closed system; it is a dynamic interaction between challenge and capacity among multiple parties within a constantly changing environment. Despite the experience of career engagement often being centered around an individual, the influences can be external, whether coming from work or another life role.

Much of the research concerning engagement, whether work, job, employee, or career, has been focused on the paid work role, with a plethora of information concerning managers and supervisors. Equally important, though perhaps not quite as much of a focus, is that of organizational leadership. In their 2011 publication, Bakker et al. noted that "the role of the leader in fostering work engagement has received limited research attention" (p. 13). In their 2015 literature review, Carasco-Saul et al. noted similar limitations, stating that "the relationship between leadership and employee engagement has not been widely investigated" (p. 38).

Yet, within the research that has been conducted, important connections are emerging. In their research exploring the role of leadership in driving engagement, Popli and Rizvi (2016) cited several studies that indicate "leadership has a critical input in fostering employee engagement" (p. 968). Similarly, Zheng et al. (2020) stated, "Several studies have shown that positive leadership styles, such as transformational leadership, serve a critical role in enhancing employee service performance" (p. 44), which would certainly be linked to engagement.

Complicating the research includes factors such as specific leadership style (e.g., transactional, ethical, servant) and what could be presumed as the leader's placement in the broader hierarchical structure of the organization. For example, using Oshry's (2007) perspective of tops (executives/senior leaders), middles (managers), and bottoms (frontline workers), there may be little interplay between a top and a bottom, making it hard to discern how much influence a truly transformative leader (top) has on a frontline worker when they may never meet. Perhaps the leadership style of the direct line manager might be a more significant influence than the style of a leader who may be several layers removed from a specific set of workers.

Organizational leaders would certainly create/influence policies that impact workers' opportunities to be engaged, but there seems to be limited research around policymakers and how their work might, ultimately, influence engagement. In this context, a policymaker would more likely be someone in government or a community stakeholder or advocate (e.g., labor groups that influence policymakers to make changes to workers' rights legislation that, in turn, impacts all workers). Patton and McMahon (2006) considered this the environmental-social system (e.g., globalization, historical influences, politics), noting this "may seem less directly related to the individual, yet their impacts can be profound" (p. 203). Individuals, families, and managers/leaders, therefore, cannot ignore the impacts policy decisions may, ultimately, have on opportunities for engagement, even when those influences may seem a world away. The COVID-19 pandemic is perhaps the most recent example, but certainly not the only one, that clearly demonstrates how connected the citizens of the world are and, in turn, how quickly global events can impact engagement.

Applying Career Engagement

As a senior leader, and the person in charge of human resources, it was Misha's responsibility to make recommendations related to the return-to-work strategy. The original lockdown had been incredibly challenging for workers across the company, but, more recently, everyone seemed to have found a good rhythm. Managers had been consistently reporting that performance and productivity often exceeded pre-pandemic levels. Yet, there needed to be some return to their head office and warehouse; in-store staff were easy as they were all very much looking forward to getting back to work and interacting with customers.

Although her grandfather was technically no longer involved in business operations, Misha was very aware that he wanted everyone back to work on-site. Not only were they paying for space, but everyone did "just fine" pre-pandemic, and he saw no reason for things to change. They all wanted to respect his view, and Misha's father felt especially pressured, but the younger family members also saw this is an opportunity to do things differently. It was especially important that they consider the matter carefully, ensuring that employees felt heard, and that their wishes and needs had all been carefully considered, regardless of whatever the final post-pandemic workspace looked like. Ultimately, Misha was strongly recommending a hybrid workplace, where staff worked remotely and on-site to varying degrees, for almost the whole organization. Her research had shown that many organizations were going in this direction (Albert, 2021; Davis, 2021; Lewis, 2021; Stahl, 2021). To begin, she focused on IT services, which had done exemplary work throughout the pandemic and had, almost seamlessly, transitioned to remote work from the very start.

In talking with Marcel (introduced in Chapter 11), Misha knew that the whole team was interested in some form of remote work, with one notable exception being Sonya (introduced in Chapter 10). After Sonya's accident, and subsequent transfer to IT, there had been quite a lot of effort to ensure she could remain with the company and continue to make a positive contribution to her team and the organization overall. They often took a job-crafting approach, which allowed Sonja to "take active steps in defining and designing their own job experience in a personally meaningful way" (Brucker & Sundar, 2020, p. 576). In terms of returning to work, Sonja wanted to craft her role in a way that would allow her to work from home almost exclusively, being fully prepared, of course, to come to head office for important team meetings/events. Marcel had indicated that Sonya's performance and productivity had improved throughout the pandemic, whereas shortly before lockdown he knew she was becoming more and more overwhelmed balancing work expectations with her health concerns, especially around pain management. From an HR perspective, Misha considered Sonya's situation different from the others as she could justify her working primarily from home as an accommodation of her disabilities. However, she strongly believed that if Sonya could work most effectively from home, then others likely could, too. She anticipated pushback from employees if they were all required to return to working on-site, and yet she didn't feel like she was prepared to upset her grandfather when he so clearly wanted everyone back. Misha knew that her father was better positioned to take an unpopular stand with her grandfather; she also knew that her father was interested in repurposing some of the office space and expanding their company to serve satellite locations in other provinces. Misha began to construct a policy proposal that would make a business case to her father about the importance of offering some employee groups flexibility about whether to work primarily on-site or from home, centering her arguments around the value of maximizing career engagement across the organization.

Activities

12.1   Understand Career/Life Engagement

As you look ahead to embedding career engagement within your organization, association, or group, take a moment to consider the perspectives of all stakeholders (e.g., clients/customers, staff, funders/investors/shareholders, community members). Record some ideas on what contributes to being overwhelmed and underutilized, as well as what career engagement means overall within your context.

Here is a sample from Misha, considering the whole organization.

What contributes to being overwhelmed?	What contributes to being underutilized?	What does "career engagement" mean?
Any large orders, especially when coupled with supplier delays, overwhelms their whole system—from sales staff to IT and the warehouse.	This can be very dependent on the location, team, and individual. I need to explore cross-training initiatives along with special projects to provide growth opportunities, when needed.	There is a positive energy with a supportive and friendly atmosphere throughout all their locations. People are bringing their "best selves" to work.

Now it's your turn.

What contributes to being overwhelmed?	What contributes to being underutilized?	What does "career engagement" mean?

12.2   Look for Synergies

Look across your organization, association, or group and identify programs/services that already exist that address career engagement.

Here is a sample from Misha.

Program/Service	Details
Health and wellness account	Although a small fund, each employee has access to a fund that supports health and wellness activities not covered by the company health plan, including purchase of personal fitness equipment and "spa days."
Tuition allowance	Each employee has access to $2,000 per year for professional development related to their position within the company.

Now it's your turn.

Program/Service	Details
. . . .	. . . .
. . . .	. . . .
. . . .	. . . .
. . . .	. . . .
. . . .	. . . .
. . . .	. . . .
. . . .	. . . .
. . . .	. . . .
. . . .	. . . .
. . . .	. . . .
. . . .	. . . .
. . . .	. . . .

As you review your list, consider what is missing (i.e., what gaps do you see?). Record your gap and craft a specific, strategic goal with a timeline for completion.

Here is a sample from Misha.

Program/Service Gap	Goal	Timeline
Tuition allowance: We need to broaden what is covered, making it easier for some employees to access learning experiences.	Write a proposal to executive that would make all or part of the allowance available for learning opportunities not specifically related to an employee's current work role.	End of Q3 2022

Now it's your turn.

Program/Service Gap	Goal	Timeline
....	....	....
....	....	....
....	....	....
....	....	....
....	....	....

12.3 Establish a Baseline

Look across your organization, association, or group and identify what engagement-related metrics you already have access to and/or those you might need to develop/implement.

Here is a sample from Misha.

Metric Name	Existing or New	Description	Value
Annual employee engagement survey	Existing	A customized engagement survey that uses the same quantitative questions each year but allows for three customized qualitative questions, ensuring a balance of longitudinal data with an ability to focus on recent events	Has proven to be well worth the expense!
Annual employee engagement survey	New	Would like to form a small employee focus group that helps develop the qualitative questions, encourages completion (though not unhappy with response rate), and shares results	Not sure yet, but confident this is a good addition to our overall strategy.

Now it's your turn.

Metric Name	Existing or New	Description	Value

12.4   Equip Leaders

Career conversations are an integral part of career engagement. Reflect on how you will equip leaders/influencers within your organization, association, or group to engage effectively in career conversations.

Here is a sample from Misha.

> Using the career engagement model as a guide, a series of training seminars will be planned to equip managers to have conversations around how engaged their team members are and, if not engaged, whether they are more likely to be overwhelmed or underutilized. They'll then explore the factors, to ensure team members feel that their work is motivating and meaningful and a good fit, along with what resources they may need.

Now it's your turn.

12.5   Recognize Limits to Capacity

Look ahead and reflect on what capacity limits you anticipate within your organization, association, or group. Some of these limits might relate to external factors, while others are internal to an individual.

Here is a sample from Misha.

External	Internal
Supply chain issues continue to be a problem	Some of the store staff do not want to return to work, or had to find work elsewhere when the stores closed.

Now it's your turn.

External	Internal
....	....
....	....
....	....
....	....

12.6   Look for Challenge Opportunities

Consider what challenge opportunities lie ahead. What can you offer the people you lead or influence?

Here is a sample from Misha.

Opportunity	Details
A more permanent, hybrid workforce may present many motivating and meaningful challenges to approach work in different ways.	IT can lead initiatives related to effective use of technologies to keep the teams connected. HR can offer managers training on effective online communication and expand the training on supporting employee mental health and well-being.

Now it's your turn.

Opportunity	Details
....	....
....	....
....	....
....	....

12.7   Watch for Disengagement

Reflect on moments when the people you lead/influence have felt overwhelmed or underutilized. Record the early warning signs and brainstorm strategies you could implement to mitigate the risk of disengagement.

Here is a sample from Misha.

Early Warning Signs	Strategies
Common signs have been centered around communication: people either being short, and almost rude, or far less communicative.	Be much more directive, but also respectful, in noting the change in behavior and asking if all is okay. Emphasize open-door policy. In the busyness of work, it is easy to just ignore or consider these signs as a "one-off" rather than a pattern.

Now it's your turn.

Early Warning Signs	Strategies

12.8   Communicate the Benefits

Consider who within your organization, association, or team will be most resistant to your career engagement goals. Compose a brief statement to address those concerns and communicate benefits. Consider what resources/evidence you might need to provide.

Here is a sample from Misha.

What is the concern?	What is your counterargument?	What resources/evidence support your case?
Grandfather is not opposed to career engagement but feels strongly that a physical return to on-site work is what it will take to get everyone fully engaged.	Despite the lockdown, business is strong, with very little dip in revenue, and engagement levels have measurably improved. Also, father has some creative plans for repurposing office spaces if we don't need as many square feet.	The most recent employee engagement survey

Now it's your turn.

What is the concern?	What is your counterargument?	What resources/evidence support your case?
....	....	....
....	....	....
....	....	....
....	....	....
....	....	....

Five Big Ideas

1. **Clarify what engagement means in your context.** Ensure employees, at all levels, understand how career engagement links to, and is different from, other forms of engagement (e.g., job, work, employee) and why career engagement works within your organization.

2. **Encourage a culture of career engagement.** Leaders at levels of your organization will need to embrace career engagement, understanding the concept and how to nurture it within themselves and their teams. Be sure to provide access to any tools, resources, and training teams may require.

3. **Establish a baseline.** To measure how (or if) career engagement efforts are making an impact, you'll need to understand where you started. Use existing survey data, conduct a separate survey, or pull from existing metrics to identify where you are now, then measure at whatever intervals make sense to your organization.

4. **Understand your systems.** Your employees exist within an individual system, influenced by factors such as their health, gender, and beliefs; a social system such as family and community; and a broader societal system, which will include socioeconomic status and geographic location. Each of these systems can influence, and be influenced by, the other, and all these factors may evolve over time.

5. **Be mindful of policy implications.** Workplace policies intended to be positive for all can, sometimes, have quite negative impacts on specific individuals. Strive for policies that leave some room to adjust for unique circumstances. Equip leaders to interpret policies, aligning to expectations while staying true to broad mission, vision, and values.

References

Albert, L. (2021, April 13). *The hybrid workplace: Engaging the post-pandemic workforce in midsize companies.* SAP. https://news.sap.com/sea/2021/04/hybrid-workplace-post-pandemic-workforce-midsize-companies/

Bakker, A., Albrecht, S. L., & Leiter, M. (2011). Key questions regarding work engagement. *European Journal of Work and Organizational Psychology, 20*(1), 4–28. https://doi.org/10.1080/1359432X.2010.485352

Brucker, D. L., & Sundar, V. (2020). Job crafting among American workers with disabilities. *Journal of Occupational Rehabilitation, 30,* 575–587. https://doi.org/10.1007/s10926-020-09889-9

Carasco-Saul, M., Kim, W., & Kim, T. (2015). Leadership and employee engagement: Proposing research agendas through a review of literature. *Human Resource Development Review, 14*(1), 38–63. https://doi.org/10.1177/1534484314560406

Davis, D. (2021). 5 models for the post-pandemic workplace. *Harvard Business Review.* https://hbr.org/2021/06/5-models-for-the-post-pandemic-workplace

Lewis, N. (2021, January 12). *Employee engagement tech key to post-pandemic success.* SHRM. https://www.shrm.org/resourcesandtools/hr-topics/technology/pages/employee-engagement-tech-key-post-pandemic-success.aspx

Oshry, B. (2007). *Seeing systems: Unlocking the mysteries of organization life* (2nd ed.). Berrett-Koehler.

Patton, W., & McMahon, M. (2006). *Career development and systems theory: Connecting theory and practice* (2nd ed.). Sense.

Popli, S., & Rizvi, I. A. (2016). Drivers of employee engagement: The role of leadership style. *Global Business Review, 17*(4), 965–979. https://doi.org/10.1177/0972150916645701

Stahl, A. (2021, April 16). *The future of offices and workspaces, post-pandemic.* Forbes. https://www.forbes.com/sites/ashleystahl/2021/04/16/the-future-of-offices-and-workspaces-post-pandemic/?sh=6f511ea56442

Zheng, Y., Graham, L., Epitropaki, O., & Snape, E. (2020). Service leadership, work engagement, and service performance: The moderating role of leader skills. *Group & Organization Management, 45*(1), 43–74. https://doi.org/10.1177/1059601119851978

Figure Credit

PART III

Beyond Career Engagement: Living Life to the Fullest

Student Engagement

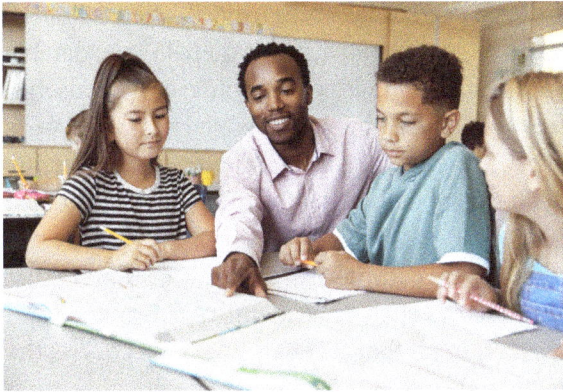

IMG. 13.1

Philippe is a Grade 5 teacher in a middle school just outside of a major urban center. The school has a fairly diverse population of students across Grades 5–8, with about 750 students in total. The school has a few portables (and more each year, it seems) and a pretty good playground space. It shares other amenities, including a track and several grass fields, with the high school. Philippe is the only male teacher in the school, which is not all that unusual, though he does find it awkward at times. His good friends, and roommates, Curt and Alfonso, are teachers at the high school and often encourage him to make the shift, but Philippe really enjoys working with the younger students.

Only 5 years beyond his teacher training, Philippe is always looking for innovative ways to inspire, excite, and engage his students in their learning. He is really committed to making a difference in their lives. At times, however, the inflexible curriculum and some senior teachers who still rely heavily on lessons from 20 years ago make Philippe wonder why he works so hard. Thankfully, these feelings don't tend to last long; he tries to use his frustrations with the system as a challenge to overcome.

Exploring Student Engagement

When it comes to the concept of engagement, the education literature seems to suffer from the same challenge as the business literature—messy, with competing definitions and approaches (Nkomo et al., 2021; Perry et al., 2010; Sinatra et al., 2015). In their 2015 literature review, Sinatra et al. noted that "there is little agreement on a concrete definition and effective measurement of engagement" (p. 1). Similarly, Reschly and Christenson (2012) stated that "engagement currently suffers from a similar problem wherein the same term is used to refer to different things ... and different terms are used for the same construct" (p. 11).

When considering engagement in education, some of the approaches include academic, social, affective, and cognitive (Finn & Zimmer, 2012); cognitive, motivational, and social-emotional (Astleitner, 2018); compliant, attentive, connected, and impassioned (Beairsto, n.d.); and behavioral, emotional, and cognitive (Perry et al., 2010; Reschly & Christenson, 2012; Sinatra et al., 2021), with the latter three seeming to be the most common. Further, according to Alrashidi et al. (2016), this is known as the "North American Model" (p. 44), and it has "been pivotal in understanding the multidimensional nature of the engagement construct" (p. 44). In their literature review, Nkomo et al. (2021) did note that "although each of the three aspects of engagement [behavioral, emotional, and cognitive] can be considered distinct, there is considerable overlap" (p. 11). Similarly, Astleitner (2018) stated, "Having these different approaches clearly shows that the dimensions of student engagement are defined in various ways with many terminological overlaps" (p. 9). In this instance, Astleitner was referring to affect, cognition, and behavior, which, again, demonstrates the different, yet also similar, terms being used.

Regardless of the competing definitions, there certainly seems to be agreement that student engagement links to important factors such as academic performance and retention (Alrashidi et al., 2016; Perry et al., 2020; Sinatra et al., 2021). Of course, the multidimensional nature of engagement, within the context of education, does seem to indicate that different approaches may have more significance on student outcomes than others (Alrashidi et al., 2016). As noted by Janosz (2012), "Thus, while we can affirm that student engagement is a major determinant of school success, we have still a lot to learn on how the different dimensions are related to it" (p. 695).

The potential links between the career engagement model and school engagement have yet to be studied, but given that *career* within the model encompasses a variety of paid and unpaid roles, including student, it seems important to consider how the dynamic interaction of challenge and capacity may impact students and educators alike. It may also make important contributions to the broader student engagement literature with regard to other life roles and the contexts in which students live and, therefore, study.

Comprising the challenge component of the career engagement model are the factors of motivating work and meaningful opportunities, both of which may connect best to the cognitive dimension of student engagement, which includes elements such as "willingness and thoughtfulness to expend the effort required to understand and master difficult tasks" (Alrashidi et al., 2016, p. 44). As the emotional dimension of student engagement is connected to motivational engagement, there may be links here as well.

Capacity, with its five factors (i.e., resources, relationships, workload, well-being, and fit) will also connect to various elements of student engagement. For example, "students exhibiting emotional engagement have a sense of identification with and belonging to the school, value school outcomes, and feel as though they are supported by their peers and teachers" (Alrashidi et al., 2016, p. 44) would align to both relationships and fit within the career engagement model.

Applying Career Engagement

In looking at his own career engagement, Philippe is confident he is almost always in the zone of engagement, recognizing that there can be ebbs and flows depending on a variety of factors. He finds his work motiving and meaningful, feels like the school is a great fit, and recognizes he has many positive relationships, at work and at home. Like many of his colleagues, Philippe finds education to be underfunded, often resulting in either students going without or teachers investing their own money to ensure students have the resources they need. Class sizes can, at times, seem larger than ideal, which, in turn, can create workload issues; however, Philippe figures he knew what he was getting into. The education system in his area has been struggling with many of these things for decades, so, as disheartening as it can be to realize things haven't changed much since he was in school, Philippe is determined to make a difference.

In thinking about the career engagement model in terms of how to engage his Grade 5 students, Philippe recognized that some of them seem underutilized and others overwhelmed. Of course, this can change according to the activity. However, he wants to take a more nuanced, customized approach to planning learning activities for his class—giving students choices so that they can each find meaning in what they need to do. He's found centering his classroom around the UN's (n.d.) Sustainable Development Goals (SDGs) has really raised some excitement this term. Each student has chosen one of the SDGs to work on across subject areas, resulting in an end-of-term project that they'll present to parents and other community stakeholders. Recognizing that all the students bring different levels of capacity to the classroom, Philippe has carefully constructed project teams, where each student can use their unique strengths. Building this community of support rather than competition and shame has made a huge difference to the energy in his class. Philippe has also paid a lot of attention to the students' well-being this year, and to his own self-care. He has initiated learning activities related to their physical and emotional health and builds in wellness breaks throughout the day.

Activities

13.1   How Did We Do Today?

A regular career engagement check-in can help students, and teachers, be mindful of when they are starting to move out of the zone of engagement toward feeling overwhelmed or underutilized. Depending on the age of the students, there are many ways this can occur; Activity 10.1, Monitor Your Career Engagement, for example, would work for older students as well as teachers.

Philippe, however, decided to take a different approach for his Grade 5 students. He elected to make a poster-size version of the model, inviting his students to identify how they were doing at the end of each day using a purple felt he kept close by. Here is what one looked like.

Career Engagement

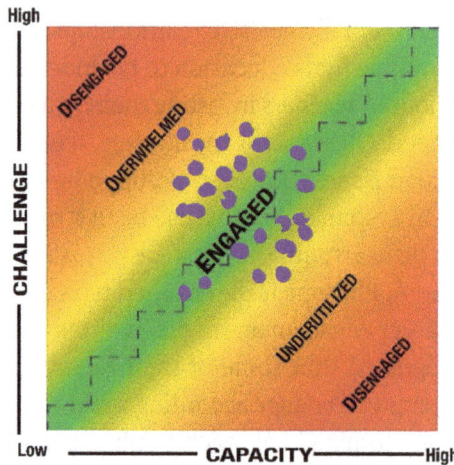

IMG. 13.2

Beside the poster, Philippe had a sheet where students could list what they found really hard (overwhelmed), what was too easy (underutilized), and what felt just right (engaged). He used simplified language as a way for students to focus on the goal of the activity rather than getting stuck in the more formal terms used in the model. Here is an example; notice how Philippe isn't concerned at this point about which students are reporting what.

Think about what we did today and what you learned. What was ...		
Really hard?	**Too easy?**	**Just about right?**
Math!!	PE; square dancing. Really???	Music was really cool today.
Math!!		Poetry
Algebra		
Square dancing is dumb		

Now it's your turn.

Career Engagement

IMG. 13.3

Think about what we did today and what you learned. What was ...		
Really hard?	**Too easy?**	**Just about right?**

Think about what we did today and what you learned. What was …

Really hard?	Too easy?	Just about right?

13.2   This Week Went …

Philippe wanted to keep a daily record of how his class was doing overall, but he also wants to know how his students are doing. He decided to do this weekly, every Wednesday. He chose midweek, giving him time to adjust, where needed, before the weekend. He simplified the language, focusing on what is or isn't working across the career engagement factors. Here is an example from one of his students.

Challenge	What's Working?	What's Not?
Motivating: I feel excited and curious	I chose SDG #6 clean water and am really excited about our project	
Meaningful: I feel like I'm learning and doing things that are important	Clean water is important. Cool project Mr. P	

Capacity	What's Working?	What's Not?
Resources: I have everything I need	I really like it when you bring in the iPad cart	
Relationships: I have someone I can talk to		My older brother is being a jerk and keeps calling me a baby cause I'm upset Pepper died

Capacity	What's Working?	What's Not?
Workload: I have enough to do		My soccer team has a tournament this weekend, so it will be hard to study for the test on Monday. Just wanted you to know.
Well-being: I am sleeping and eating properly, getting some exercise, feeling well		My cat died
Fit: I feel included and heard, that I matter	I like our project team, and making new friends, too!	

Select one of the areas that isn't working well; identify one thing we could do to improve.

Everything seems okay this week, Mr. P. except our cat died on Sunday, and I'm feeling pretty sad. She'd been around my whole life and often slept on my pillow. It is kind of hard to concentrate.

Now it's your turn.

Challenge	What's Working?	What's Not?
Motivating: I feel excited and curious	....	....
	....	....
	....	....
	....	....
Meaningful: I feel like I'm learning and doing things that are important	....	....
	....	....
	....	....
	....	....

Capacity	What's Working?	What's Not?
Resources: I have everything I need	....	....
Relationships: I have someone I can talk to	....	....
Workload: I have enough to do	....	....
Well-being: I am sleeping and eating properly, getting some exercise, feeling well	....	....
Fit: I feel included and heard, that I matter	....	....

Select one of the areas that isn't working well; identify one thing we could do to improve.

Five Big Ideas

1. **Consider the class, each student, and yourself.** Career engagement is an individual experience, but each individual's experience will influence the whole and, in turn, the whole will influence each individual. Be mindful of creating an environment that maximizes engagement for all.

2. **Remember to provide adequate scaffolding.** Vygotsky's (1978) zone of proximal development is like a "sweet spot"—the place where learning can occur with adequate support. Recognize when that support is needed and when sufficient foundation exists for students to learn more independently.

3. **Honor and embrace diversity.** Students and educators will come from diverse communities, including race, culture, ethnicity, language, gender, and socio-economic status. Students will also have preferences or aptitudes for different subject areas, from the math whiz and writer to the athlete and artist. Provide opportunities for their uniqueness to shine.

4. **Be mindful of the systems influencing you and your students.** Every aspect of the career engagement model will be impacted by the systems you are a part of, especially those that influence education such as governments, teacher associations/unions, communities, and parents, all of whom have a stake in how education is delivered, how students are engaged, and what outcomes are measured.

5. **Student engagement doesn't have to be hard.** By focusing on the unique individual and contextual capacity of each student, and providing challenges that align with that capacity (recognizing that changes in capacity can shift from one moment to the next), optimal engagement is both possible and sustainable.

References

Alrashidi, O., Phan, H. P., & Ngu, B. H. (2016). Academic engagement: An overview of its definitions, dimensions, and major conceptualisations. *International Education Studies, 9*(12), 41–52. https://files.eric.ed.gov/fulltext/EJ1121524.pdf

Astleitner, H. (2018). Multidimensional engagement in learning: As integrated instructional design approach. *Journal of Instructional Research, 7.* https://files.eric.ed.gov/fulltext/EJ1188334.pdf

Beairsto, B. (n.d.). *Engagement in learning: Finding the depth beyond diligence.* The Critical Thinking Consortium. https://tc2.ca/uploads/PDFs/Critical%20Discussions/engagement_in_learning.pdf

Finn, J. D., & Zimmer, K.S. (2012). Student engagement: What is it? Why does it matter? In S. L. Christenson, A. L. Reschly, & C. Wylie (Eds.), *Handbook of research on student engagement* (pp. 97–131). Springer.

Janosz., M. (2012). Part IV commentary: Outcomes of engagement and engagement as an outcome: Some consensus, divergences, and unanswered questions. In S. L. Christenson, A. L. Reschly, & C. Wylie (Eds), *Handbook of research on student engagement* (pp. 695–705). Springer.

Nkomo, L. M., Daniel, B. K., & Butson, R. J. (2021). Synthesis of student engagement with digital technologies: A systematic review of the literature. *International Journal of Educational Technology in Higher Education, 18,* 1–26. https://doi.org/10.1186/s41239-021-00270-1

Perry, J. C., Liu, X., & Pabian, Y. (2010). School engagement as a mediator of academic performance among urban youth: The role of career preparation, parental career support, and teacher support. *The Counseling Psychologist, 38,* 269–295. https://doi.org/10.1177/0011000009349272

Reschly, A. L., & Christenson, S. L. (2012). Jingle, jangle, and conceptual haziness: Evolution and future direction of the engagement construct. In S. L. Christenson, A. L. Reschly, & C. Wylie (Eds), *Handbook of research on student engagement* (pp. 3–19). Springer.

Sinatra, G. M., Heddy, B. C., & Lombardi, D. (2015). The challenges of defining and measuring student engagement in science. *Educational Psychologist, 50*(1), 1–13. https://doi.org/10.1080/00461520.2014.1002924

United Nations. (n.d.). *Sustainable development goals.* https://sdgs.un.org/goals

Vygotsky, L. S. (1978). *Mind and society: The development of higher psychological processes* (M. Cole, V. John-Steiner, S. Scribner, & E. Souberman, Eds.). Harvard University Press. https://doi.org/10.2307/j.ctvjf9vz4

Figure Credits

CHAPTER FOURTEEN

Family Engagement

IMG. 14.1

Julio, now 32, had devoted his life to his sport. His parents, sister, and other extended family members had all made great sacrifices, personally and professionally, to help him succeed. Over the years, the family had relocated several times to live closer to the schools, training programs, teams, or coaches that could take Julio to the next level. They'd pooled financial resources to pay for his training, equipment, and travel, as well as to support his day-to-day living expenses so that he didn't need a paying job. Julio had competed at the Olympics three times and decided that the Tokyo Summer Olympics in 2021 would be his last competition. His whole family was heartbroken when the tough decision was made to proceed without any spectators due to the COVID-19 pandemic; however, they were incredibly proud of him and had no regrets about helping him reach this career highlight. After the Olympics, though, everyone realized that it was time to shift the family's attention and support into a new direction as Julio's maternal grandparents were no longer able to care for themselves in their own home and Julio's younger sister, Eloa, had just been accepted to grad school. Both his grandparents and his sister were moving into Julio's parents' home. It was time for Julio to move out and find work that would help him to pay his own way and give back to the family who had so unconditionally supported him for the past 32 years.

Exploring Family Engagement

The notion of family engagement is relatively new but is an important consideration, especially for individuals who identify with the values of a collectivist culture. Similar to workplace engagement, where the diverse needs of many different employees need to be met within the context of keeping the organization viable and sustainable, family engagement is complex; there are many unique, and sometimes conflicting, needs to consider. Research has demonstrated that parental engagement with a child tacitly signals that child's self-worth and, in part because of that, contributes to the child's later career adaptability and persistence (Amarnani et al., 2018). Julio's Olympic dreams would have been far out of reach without his parents' involvement and belief in him throughout his athletic career; most important was Julio's *perception* of his parents' support and engagement. He knew without a doubt that they loved and supported him unconditionally.

For many individuals from collectivist cultures, family support goals (i.e., wanting to help their family) are their most important motivators, predicting both optimal learning outcomes and engagement (King & McInerney, 2019). Rallying around Julio's Olympic dreams, therefore, likely served as a significant goal for the extended family, engaging them all in supporting his amazing success. Even Julio's sister's career likely benefitted from this; given her desire to be successful to support the family, she would have been more focused at school and in her career, fueling her own professional achievement. Within the context of collectivist cultures, the family system operates as a unit; "therefore, to introduce anything, all family members in that system must agree" (Sumari et al., 2020, p. 400). Julio's family agreed, implicitly or explicitly, to support his Olympic goals; as he retired from his Olympic career, the family's focus shifted to supporting his sister, Eloa's, academic goals, concurrently with their shared goal of supporting Julio and Eloa's grandparents. Functional collectivist families are cohesive, guided by shared values, and engage in open communication and negotiation (Sumari et al., 2020). Open, healthy communication, in turn contributes to well-being (Kiyama et al., 2015), a key capacity factor in the career engagement model. In the past, especially within individualistic Western cultural contexts, the role of parents and families in a young adult's education or career had been questioned—often interpreted as intrusive, pushy, or overly protective; increasingly, however, family engagement is understood as supportive and contributing to the academic and career success of each other (Kiyama et al., 2015).

There are many different family structures that the career engagement model can be useful for. For example, the career development of women is often influenced by whether they choose to have children and, if they do choose to start a family, their commitment to, and perceived salience of, their mothering role (Ussher et al., 2016). In Julio's case, his mother likely set aside her own career growth and development each time the family moved to strengthen Julio's chances for Olympic success. Much has also been written on the experiences of dual career couples (Neault, 2008; Neault & Pickerell, 2005), accompanying partners (Reichrath-Smith & Neault, 2013), and work–life conflicts (Blair & Obradovic, 2018; Duxbury & Higgins, 2003, 2009, 2012). Career engagement doesn't occur in isolation; within any family system, the career aspirations and decisions of one member impact, and are impacted by, the career aspirations and decisions of the others.

Applying Career Engagement

We can examine engagement in Julio's scenario from both his individual perspective and the perspective of the family as a whole.

At an individual level, Julio will likely find it difficult to realign his levels of challenge and capacity after such a long and rewarding career as an Olympic athlete. He will need a high level of challenge, in terms of meaningful work and motivating opportunities, to remain fully engaged. However, it may be next to impossible to find work that fully utilizes the specific skills he's honed for so many years, and he'll need to develop new skills for whatever type of work he pursues. Regardless of the role he takes on, he'll almost certainly find his skills as an elite athlete underutilized. He may find it over-whelming to seek out work as he's never had to apply for a job before. He'll also need to learn about the culture and expectations of more traditional workplaces, perhaps finding it hard to fit into a more typical work structure. Being too overwhelmed or too underutilized can, of course, result in disengagement. It will be important for Julio to take strategic steps to shift into a post-Olympics rhythm of work and other life roles.

Julio's extended family, however, will also be impacted by his retirement from Olympic competition. For 20-plus years many of the family decisions and most of their financial resources have revolved around supporting Julio; although he's grateful for that, he knows he can never adequately repay them. As a family, sustaining optimal engagement has required an ever-adjusting alignment between challenge and capacity. In many ways, they had all lived vicariously through Julio's Olympic successes; their own work, caregiving responsibilities, and financial commitments, although challenging, felt both meaningful and motivating as they contributed to a shared family Olympic goal. At times, their combined capacity had been stretched, but life had generally stayed manageable as they worked together to support each other, with Julio's Olympic dreams at the center of their focus. They spelled each other off in terms of workload; sometimes one family member worked at two jobs so another could be free to travel with Julio, especially in his younger years. Mentally and emotionally the whole family was doing well; their relationships were strong, and they all agreed that being part of Julio's Olympic career was a great fit.

Now that Julio is retiring from his Olympic career, however, the whole family system will begin to shift. At the moment, their new focus will be caring for Julio's grandparents and welcoming them into the family home. They are all also excited about Julio's sister, Eloa's, acceptance to grad school; she'll be the first "doctor" in the family, even though it will be as an academic rather than in medicine. Although neither of these changes are as exciting or all-consuming as pursuing an Olympic dream, they're motivating and meaningful to each member of Julio's family, and together they'll find a way to make it work. Pursuing an Olympic dream is expensive; with Julio's retirement there will be less overall financial strain. However, there will also be a temporary but significant loss in monthly income for the family until Eloa's salary as an investment advisor is replaced, at least in part, once Julio starts working. There will be less family time spent watching Julio compete, so the family wants to find a project to work on together; they're thinking of building a cabin on property that they'll purchase once Julio's grandparents sell their home. They recognize that there will be ups and downs ahead but are committed to keeping their family connected and pooling their resources to maximize everyone's opportunity to thrive.

Activities

14.1   Family Visioning

Shared goals and open communication are key elements of family engagement, along with an alignment of challenge and capacity. Lewin's (1938) forcefield analysis approach can be useful in collectively analyzing what's pushing the family toward the shared vision as well as what roadblocks remain in their way.

To complete a forcefield analysis, begin by writing your shared family *vision* in the space at the top. Next, consider what motivators are fueling your individual and combined desire to achieve that vision. Record those as *positive forces* in the diagram (lower arrows). Also consider what might block you from bringing your shared vision to life. Record *negative forces* in the diagram (upper arrows).

Review your completed diagram and identify which of the positive and negative forces are within your combined power to change. Identify a few *roadblocks* (negative forces working against you) to tackle and get out of the way. Also identify a few *strengths* (positive forces motivating you) to focus on; this will offer the turbo boost needed to blast your way past the barriers to achieving your shared vision.

Here is a sample from Julio.

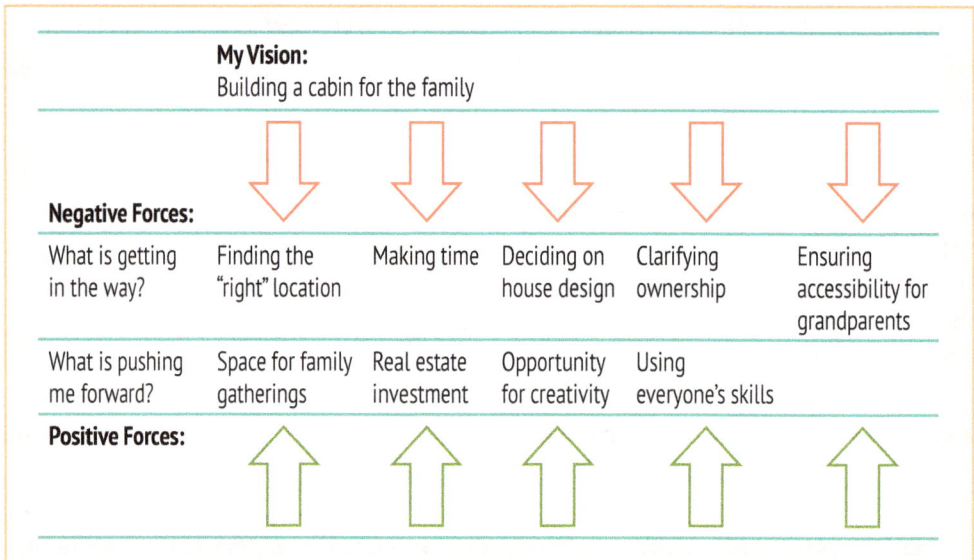

My Vision: Building a cabin for the family					
Negative Forces:					
What is getting in the way?	Finding the "right" location	Making time	Deciding on house design	Clarifying ownership	Ensuring accessibility for grandparents
What is pushing me forward?	Space for family gatherings	Real estate investment	Opportunity for creativity	Using everyone's skills	
Positive Forces:					

| Roadblocks | Ensuring accessibility for grandparents may be a challenge, but because we're starting from the beginning, we can consult with an architect who has experience with accessibility design. |
| Strengths | Involving the family earlier on in the design process provides the opportunity for everyone to get involved and use their skills (and creativity). I hope to build long-lasting memories. |

Now it's your turn.

My Vision:

Negative Forces:

What is getting in the way?

What is pushing me forward?

Positive Forces:

Roadblocks

Strengths

14.2   Asset Mapping

In times of significant transitions, for individuals, families, or community groups, it can be helpful to take stock of all the assets available as you formulate a clear vision and develop an action plan to get there. Asset mapping (Improvement and Development Agency, 2009) is a tool that can support this important stage.

As a sample, here's what Julio pulled together when the family met to discuss what they each had to contribute to building a cabin.

Individuals	<ul><li>Eloa: Financial (investments)</li><li>Grandfather: Creative (architect)</li><li>Dad: Technical (trades)</li><li>Mom: Technical (sewing)</li><li>Grandmother: Creative (paintings/décor)</li></ul>
Associations	
Organizations	<ul><li>Uncle's construction business: Might donate time for a share of the investment</li></ul>
Physical	<ul><li>Furniture and appliances (i.e., from grandparents' home)</li><li>Physical resort just 2 hours away from where they all live; buying now will be a good long-term investment</li></ul>
Economic	<ul><li>Money from the sale of the grandparents' property</li></ul>
Cultural	

Now it's your turn.

Individuals	....
Associations	....
Organizations	....
Physical	....
Economic	....
Cultural	....

Five Big Ideas

1. **You're not in this alone.** Within families, career and life decisions are rarely made in isolation. To optimize family engagement, keep the lines of communication open, share goals and dreams, and work together to make the needed adjustments to bring those dreams to life.

2. **Systems shift.** Systems theories (Patton & McMahon, 2006) tell us that even the smallest shift in one part of a family system will impact other parts of the system, sometimes in a pretty big way. This is why adaptability and flexibility are so important to keep family engagement at an optimal level. Offer the family as much lead time as possible to help them prepare for known changes and foster resilience to handle the times when unexpected shifts happen as, of course, they will!

3. **Pass the baton.** In dual career couples, and other family constellations, everyone's career and life goals can't be the primary focus at the same time. Successful couples and families take turns in terms of whose career is the priority. To maximize family engagement, be sure to pass the baton (and offer support) to the next person when it's their turn to shine.

4. **Contribute what you can.** Recognize that each member of the family is also part of intersecting systems beyond the family and won't be able to equally contribute time, energy, or more tangible resources. Aim for equity rather than equality. When deciding how much you can contribute, reflect on your own limits in terms of both challenge and capacity. You'll contribute more to family engagement if you're able to follow through with your commitments than if you overcommit and end up burned out or resentful.

5. **Celebrate successes.** To maximize family engagement, join together in celebrating successes—even the small ones. Acknowledge with gratitude the contributions of each family member, even if the success is seen externally as an individual accomplishment. Ensure that everyone knows how their unique contribution, however small, contributed to the ultimate outcome.

References

Amarnani, R. K., Garcia, P. R. J. M., Restubog, S. L. D., Bordia, P., & Bordia, S. (2018). Do you think I'm worth it? The self-verifying role of parental engagement in career adaptability and career persistence among STEM students. *Journal of Career Assessment, 26*(1), 77–94. https://doi.org/10.1177/1069072716679925

Blair, S. L., & Obradovic, J. (Eds.). (2018). *The work-family interface: Spillover, complications, and challenges.* Emerald.

Duxbury, L., & Higgins, C. (2003). *Work-life conflict in Canada in the new millennium: A status report.* Health Canada. https://publications.gc.ca/collections/Collection/H72-21-186-2003E.pdf

Duxbury, L., & Higgins, C. (2009). *Work–life conflict in Canada in the new millennium: Key findings and recommendations from the 2001 national work–life conflict study* (*Report Six*). Health Canada. http://www.hc-sc.gc.ca/ewh-semt/alt_formats/hecs-sesc/pdf/pubs/occup-travail/balancing_six-equilibre_six/balancing_six-equilibre_six-eng.pdf

Duxbury, L., & Higgins, C. (2012). *Revisiting work-life issues in Canada: The 2012 national study on balancing work and caregiving in Canada.* http://newsroom.carleton.ca/wp-content/files/2012-National-Work-Long-Summary.pdf

Improvement and Development Agency. (2009). *A glass half-full: How an asset approach can improve community health and well-being.* http://www.assetbasedconsulting.net/uploads/publications/A%20glass%20half%20full.pdf

King, R. B., & McInerney, D. M. (2019). Family-support goals drive engagement and achievement in a collectivist context: Integrating etic and emic approaches in goal research. *Contemporary Educational Psychology, 58*, 338–353. https://doi.org/10.1016/j.cedpsych.2019.04.003

Kiyama, J. M., Harper, C. E., Ramos, D., Aguayo, D., Page, L. A., & Riester, K. A. (2015). Parent and family engagement in higher education. *ASHE Higher Education Report, 41*(6), 1–94. https://doi.org/10.1002/aehe.20024

Lewin, K. (1938). *The conceptual representation and the measurement of psychological forces.* Duke University Press. https://doi.org/10.1037/13613-000

Neault, R. (2008). Todd and Naomi: Dual career transitions. In N. Arthur, & P. Pedersen (Eds.)., *Case incidents in counseling for international transitions.* American Counseling Association.

Neault, R. A., & Pickerell, D. A. (2005). Professional women in dual career families: The juggling act. *Canadian Journal of Counselling, 39*(3), 187–198. https://cjc-rcc.ucalgary.ca/article/view/58761/44248

Patton, W., & McMahon, M. (2006). *Career development and systems theory: Connecting theory and practice* (2nd ed.). Sense.

Reichrath-Smith, C., & Neault, R. A. (2013). The global careerist: Internal and external supports needed for success. *Journal of the National Institute for Career Education and Counselling, 31*, 51–58. https://hubble-live-assets.s3.amazonaws.com/nicec/redactor2_assets/files/82/NICEC_Journal_31_Oct_2013.pdf

Sumari, M., Baharudin, D. F., Khalid, N. M., Ibrahim, N. H., & Ahmed Tharbe, I. H. (2020). Family functioning in a collectivist culture of Malaysia: A qualitative study. *The Family Journal, 28*(4), 396–402. https://doi.org/10.1177/1066480719844334

Ussher, S., Roche, S., & Cable, D. (2016). Women and careers: New Zealand women's engagement in career and family planning. *New Zealand Journal of Employment Relations, 40*(3), 24–43. http://www.nzjournal.org/NZJER40%283%29.pdf

Figure Credit

CHAPTER FIFTEEN

Community Engagement

IMG. 15.1

Elli-Anne, Jacob, and their three children (Eliza [11], Jonah [8], and Salome [6]) were all actively involved in their local community, where Jacob's family had lived for three generations. Elli-Anne enjoyed her role on the Community Fair Days committee; Jacob served on the board of the Business Improvement Association; and Eliza, Jonah, and Salome were all in the 4H club. Jacob and Elli-Anne both played key roles within their church community and, on top of all that, Elli-Anne homeschooled all three of their children, which involved active engagement with the homeschooling association and weekly community classes and co-op projects. Their lives were happy, and their days were full. When Jacob was offered a huge promotion by his employer, which would require relocating to another city on the other side of the country, each member of the family was devastated; none of them wanted to move. However, after carefully considering the opportunity and talking it over with family, friends, and other trusted advisors, Jacob and Elli-Anne felt strongly called to accept the promotion. After discussing the pros and cons of the move with their children, the family decided to make the big move and to embark on this new adventure together.

Exploring Community Engagement

The notion of community engagement has often been linked with activism or disruption at a grassroots level to advocate for and initiate change (Giloth, 2018). Community engagement is also a focus within career development and cooperative learning initiatives, intended to provide individuals with an inside look at an occupation, industry, or organization, sometimes with mentorship or structured work experiences (Finkel, 2017). Sometimes community engagement is conceptualized as civic engagement, which can include volunteering, political participation, financial contributions, and membership in community organizations and associations (Li, 2020), Within the career engagement model, we are looking at community engagement broadly to include voluntary, leisure, and learning activities that offer connections to the community and meaningful opportunities that inspire motivation. Certainly advocacy, social justice, and values-driven initiatives fit within this description (Giloth, 2018); however, so does joining an interest-based club, volunteering to help with a neighborhood block party, engaging in a work-integrated learning experience, or contributing to a community garden.

Relocation, not surprisingly, disrupts community engagement, especially in terms of social connections. In a study of military members and their families, who are known for relocating often, O'Neal et al. (2020) found that community connections were linked to both individual and family coping and well-being. Praharso et al. (2017) also looked at stressful life events, including relocation, finding that the loss of social identity negatively impacted well-being, making it important to make new community connections as part of reconstructing one's social identity and optimizing well-being.

Li (2020) found that increased community engagement was positively associated with mental health and satisfaction with life; both would fit under the career engagement model's well-being factor. Several other researchers have investigated the links between community involvement and well-being in older adults. For example, after a forced relocation in China, researchers found that community participation positively affected the adjustment of older women (Zhang, 2019), which could, in turn, be considered part of their well-being. Similarly, in research with older adults, membership in a community group contributed to their social well-being (Lindsay-Smith et al., 2018).

The key to optimal community engagement, just as with other types of engagement, is to effectively align the level of challenge to available capacity rather than over- or under-committing. Community engagement both relies on, and can boost, an individual's capacity. For example, after relocating, individuals lose much of their social support network. By actively engaging within their new community, they could begin to rebuild a network of friends and resourceful people to turn to in challenging moments. However, their value to the organizations they support is linked to their previous experiences and the transferable skills and competencies they bring to their new roles. Community engagement can be a win-win proposition, even when that isn't always the primary focus.

Research has also examined links between spiritual resources and work engagement. Interestingly, overly focusing on the engagement of workers within spiritual organizations can diminish, rather than optimize their spiritual resources; the spiritual aspects can become less of a focus than the work aspects (Bickerton et al., 2014). Although not specifically addressed, it's not a stretch to think that this could also apply to volunteers within faith-based organizations. Within the career engagement model, it's essential, therefore, to keep the focus on meaning, aligning challenges with the spiritual values that are underlying an individual's motivation to serve.

Applying Career Engagement

The Johnsons were surrounded by love at the many goodbye events prior to their move; the kids had sleepovers with close friends and special times with their cousins. Finding new homes for many of their animals had been the hardest; the family had decided to turn the travel to their new home into a cross-country road trip, so they agreed that all pets except the family dog would need to be given away.

Each in their own way, the Johnsons would have all been considered optimally engaged in their community prior to the move, and very socially connected. They each had challenging roles that were uniquely matched to their individual and combined capacities. The trip across the country was a fantastic adventure for all of them and provided 6 weeks of bonding for the family. Life was good!

However, once they arrived in their new city, things started to get tougher. Jacob's job was challenging, leaving less time for the family and no time at all to seek out a business association in the community. Although Eli-Anne continued to homeschool the children, it felt lonely and more challenging without the weekly connections with other homeschooling families and friends. The family had all been excited to go to their new church, but it just didn't feel the same; nobody knew them, and it felt weird to be participants rather than leaders. Although people were friendly and welcoming, that seemed to make it worse, amplifying all that they'd left behind.

The career engagement model emphasizes the importance of matching capacity to challenge. In the Johnsons' case, they were concurrently experiencing being over-whelmed and underutilized. There was tension at home and, by fall, the closeness they'd experienced as a family traveling across the country in the summer was starting to unravel.

To achieve and sustain optimal engagement, adjustments needed to be made to both challenge and capacity. After settling into their new home and beginning another homeschooling year, the Johnsons realized that their top priority was to build connec-tions and to find ways to serve in a meaningful way within their new community. This type of involvement would also help to replenish their capacity; by moving across the country, they'd lost the day-to-day in-person supports of close friends, family mem-bers, and even the children's pets. Everything was new and strange; each basic task like finding groceries in the store took longer, and they had to adjust to a new doctor, dentist, and even hairstylist!

Jacob and Elli-Anne decided to start by making a game out of getting to know their community, engaging their children in another adventure of discovery. They began by making a list of the local community centers and recreational facilities, bookmarking on the family computer the various calendars of fall events. As part of the children's homeschooling activities, Elli-Anne assigned Eliza the task of making a list of local business associations and service clubs for their dad to consider, with a brief summary and contact info for each. Jonah and Salome were each given smaller projects; Jonah had to research the local pet shelters to see if there were any volunteer opportunities for children, and Salome went through the family photo album on the computer to choose pictures to print of all of the friends, family members, and pets that they missed, so that they could make a collage for the fridge. They also agreed to try to find one family at church next Sunday that they could invite out to a restaurant for lunch.

By the end of the year, the Johnsons were beginning to feel settled and engaged in their new community. Jacob was attending monthly Chamber of Commerce meetings, Elli-Anne was involved in a homeschooling association, Eliza was enrolled in dance lessons and, through Jonah's research, the family was fostering kittens for the local animal shelter. Jonah and Salome were both in the junior choir at church and enjoying their swimming lessons. Through their community activities, they were building new friendships and support systems and, each in their own way, engaged in meaningful, motivating activities. Life was once again good!

Activities

15.1   Mapping Community Resources

Begin to map out specific community resources within your community by asking friends, colleagues, neighbors; looking at community directories, groups, community boards; or searching online in your area. Consider completing the asset mapping exercise introduced in Chapter 14 first to start your thinking.

Here is a sample from the Johnsons. They pulled together a list and overlaid that on a map of the area.

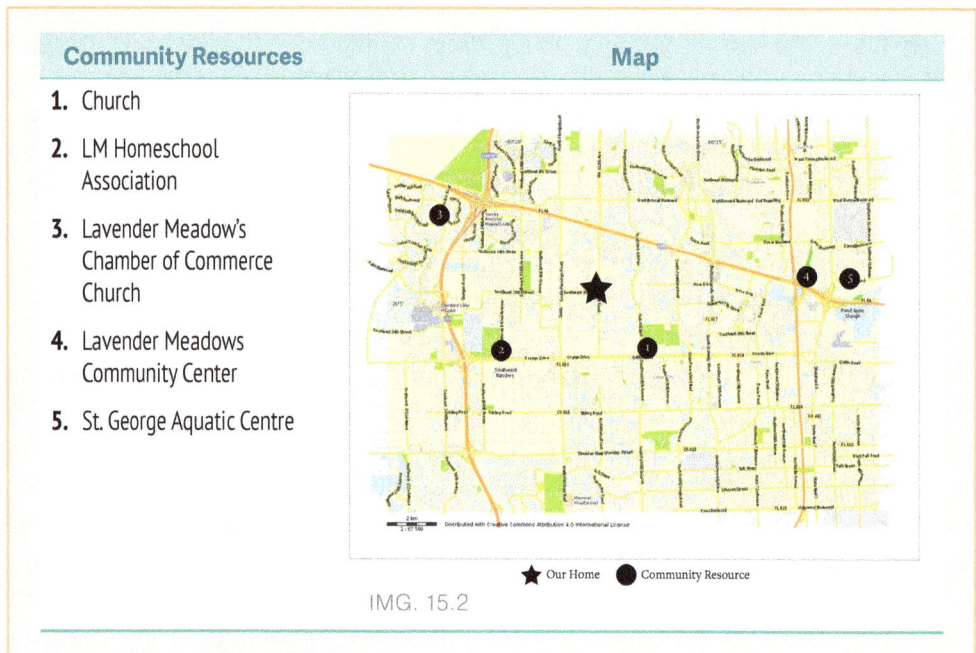

Community Resources	Map
1. Church	
2. LM Homeschool Association	
3. Lavender Meadow's Chamber of Commerce Church	
4. Lavender Meadows Community Center	
5. St. George Aquatic Centre	

★ Our Home   ● Community Resource

IMG. 15.2

Now it's your turn.

Community Resources	Map
1.	
2.	
3.	
4.	
5.	
6.	
7.	
8.	

Note: You can map out our neighborhood on Google maps or a printout of your local area.

15.2   Getting to Know You

With your map in hand, the next step will be to follow up with specific community resources to determine how they can best support you or how you can contribute to them in some way.

Here is a sample from the Johnsons where Eliza was tasked with making a list of local business associations and service clubs for her dad to consider, with a brief summary and contact info for each.

Community Resource	Lavender Meadow's Chamber of Commerce (LMCC)
Description	The mission of LMCC is to support local business to grow and thrive within the community. They offer a wide variety of resources targeted at setting up and running a business, as well as monthly networking events. The LMCC logo is visible on many of the shops we've visited within our area.
Location	684 Lilac Drive, Lavender Meadows
Website	www.lavendermeadowschamber.com
Contact Name	Pepper Maximo **Phone** 450-xxx-2222 ext. 5 **Email** pepper.maximo@lmcc.net
Information Needed	• How much does membership cost? • Can I attend meetings without being a member? • Do you have a mentorship program?

Now it's your turn.

Community Resource

....

....

....

....

Description

....

....

....

....

Location

....

....

....

....

Website ....

....

....

....

Contact Name   **Phone** ....   **Email** ....

....

....

....

Information   ....
Needed
....

....

....

Five Big Ideas

1. **Know yourself.** Recognize how much, or how little, you need to be with others to feel optimally engaged. There are many meaningful ways to contribute to your community, regardless of your preference for working alone or in a group.
2. **Know your community.** Asset mapping can be a good starting place. Make a list of the types of resources or programs that interest you and then begin a virtual or in-person scavenger hunt to discover all that your community has to offer.
3. **Find meaningful, motivating opportunities.** Optimal engagement is far more than busyness. Don't simply say yes to every invitation. Instead, listen to your inner voice and engage in activities that you find personally meaningful and will be motivated to contribute to.
4. **Be strategic.** Community involvement can serve multiple purposes. Take time to assess the needs of your community or the expectations of the specific organization that you'd like to join or contribute to. Compare their needs to your

own purpose for engaging with them. Optimal engagement isn't one-sided; take time to find a good match between the specific challenges that you choose to take on and the capacity that you have within you to give.

5. **Plan gracious exits.** Sometimes it's hard to withdraw from volunteer activities or community commitments. It shouldn't take a cross-country move to release you from responsibilities, so be clear about what you're taking on, for how long, and how to transition the next person into your role.

References

Bickerton, G. R., Miner, M. H., Dowson, M., & Griffin, B. (2014). Spiritual resources and work engagement among religious workers: A three-wave longitudinal study. *Journal of Occupational and Organizational Psychology, 87*, 370–391. https://doi.org/10.1111/joop.12052

Finkel, L. (2017). Walking the path together from high school to STEM majors and careers: Utilizing community engagement and a focus on teaching to increase opportunities for URM students. *Journal of Science Education and Technology, 26*(1), 116–126. https://www.jstor.org/stable/45151196

Giloth, R. (2018). Philanthropy and community engagement. *National Civic Review, 107*(2), 26–36. https://doi.org/10.1002/ncr.21361

Li, Y. (2020). Civic engagement and wellbeing among female immigrants in Canada. *Canadian Ethnic Studies, 52*(1), 49–72. https://doi.org/10.1353/ces.2020.0006

Lindsay-Smith, G., O'Sullivan, G., Eime, R., Harvey, J., & van Uffelen, J. G Z. (2018). A mixed methods case study exploring the impact of membership of a multi-activity, multicentre community group on social wellbeing of older adults. *BMC Geriatrics, 18*(1), 226–226. https://doi.org/10.1186/s12877-018-0913-1

O'Neal, C. W., Richardson, E. W., & Mancini, J. A. (2020). Community, context, and coping: How social connections influence coping and well-being for military members and their spouses. *Family Process, 59*(1), 158–172. https://doi.org/10.1111/famp.12395

Praharso, N. F., Tear, M. J., & Cruwys, T. (2017). Stressful life transitions and wellbeing: A comparison of the stress buffering hypothesis and the social identity model of identity change. *Psychiatry Research, 247*, 265–275. https://doi.org/10.1016/j.psychres.2016.11.039

Zhang, J. (2019). How community participation promotes the relocation adjustment of older women: A moderated mediation analysis. *Social Indicators Research, 143*(2), 637–655. https://doi.org/10.1007/s11205-018-2006-0

Figure Credits

Retirement Engagement

IMG. 16.1

Abdul, now 63, had originally retired from his role at a structural engineering consultancy firm at the age of 60, after having what many considered a dream job there for 30-plus years. His projects had spanned four continents, but "home" had always been in London. For the 1st year post-retirement, Abdul had enjoyed extensive international travel, revisiting family and work colleagues whom he hadn't seen for years, as his last 5-year project had been in a remote part of China and any time off from there had been spent back in the UK.

However, then the COVID-19 pandemic grounded travel all around the world. Abdul worked on long overdue projects in his own London townhome, as well as helping to care for his aging parents who were still in their own family home. He also financially supported his brother's family business, a small Middle Eastern restaurant on the outskirts of London, which had been closed for much of the past year during lockdowns. Although some restaurants had pivoted to takeout food and patio dining, neither option was feasible due to the location of this restaurant. After much consultation and, with a great deal of shame and distress, Abdul's brother and his family decided to close their restaurant, with no capacity to repay Abdul's loan.

The financial loss, coupled with growing boredom while grounded at home doing minor renovations, motivated Abdul to reconsider his retirement plans. Like many retirees, Abdul recognized that he still had much more to give, professionally as well as personally. He also wanted to replenish some of the retirement savings that he'd spent trying to help his brother. Returning to work of some kind started to take on a greater appeal.

Exploring Retirement Engagement

For many aging adults who are contemplating retirement, their core requirement for continuing to work is flexibility and more control over their time (Luke & Neault, 2020). Straughan and Tadai (2018), in their Singaporean research on flexiwork options, reported that, although a commitment to the principles of a flexible workplace may be widely endorsed by government leaders, employers, and employees, these principles are often not laid out in policies that can be reasonably implemented. Their study participants reported that, even if being paid for part-time work, the demands on their time equated to full-time. They expressed a mix of guilt and gratitude for their "privileged" status; the researchers concluded, however, that the flexiworkers were better described as "marginalized" and had not been fairly remunerated for their contributions. Clearly this has impact on the motivation of retired workers (or those eligible to retire); if money is not their primary motivation for working, then most want to be paid fairly for the time that they commit to the workforce or they would prefer not to work at all, preserving their time to engage in other meaningful activities.

An exception to money or flexibility as motivators for post-retirement work, however, may be workers who have considered their work a calling or vocation. This fits with the career engagement notion of meaningful work. In their research, Ronkainen et al. (2020) found that many older sports coaches, for example, were more likely to continue coaching out of a sense of duty and to leave a legacy. Matz-Costa et al. (2014) also defined engagement as a subjective experience rather than simply participating in something; regardless of role, older workers were more engaged if they perceived purpose and meaning in their contributions (i.e., creating something or providing a needed service rather than engaging in activities solely to benefit themselves). Work values, especially those like self-transcendence that focused on benefitting others, can also predict post-retirement work (Wöhrmann et al., 2016).

Interestingly, Hamm and his colleagues (2019) found that workers who had been most engaged pre-retirement were the most likely to remain engaged across other life roles. Retaining engaged older workers, therefore, can be a struggle—even if they find work a good fit, meaningful, motivating, and fulfilling social and emotional needs, engaged workers know that they will be able to find similar satisfaction and motivation as they optimize their engagement in other key roles. The same researchers found, however, that retirees who had low work engagement pre-retirement maintained that status post-retirement. They were less likely to volunteer, return to work part-time, or even take on additional household chores, although they maintained high engagement in other life domains such as with children or spouses.

Age discrimination adds another layer of complexity in understanding the motivations of older adults to continue to work, or to return to work post-retirement (Bayl-Smith & Griffin, 2014). Clearly, for older adults who have choices about whether to continue to work, being discriminated against may tip the skills toward leaving the workforce; Bayl-Smith and Griffen found a negative relationship between discrimination and work engagement, suggesting that it would be less likely for older workers to stay in the workforce if they felt devalued and discriminated against. However, in many countries worldwide, there is an increasing need to keep older adults working—in part to fill labor market shortages and facilitate knowledge transfer, but also to address the economic realities of the inability for governments or corporate pension plans to adequately fund lengthy retirements (Bayl-Smith & Griffin, 2014). Therefore, it is increasingly important to understand the motivations of older workers and to equip workplaces to attract, retain, and fully engage them (Luke et al., 2016).

Canadian retirement specialist Nell Smith (2014) developed the six circles of life model to support taking a holistic look at the needs of older adults. The model begins with "Be who you are," which focuses on reflecting and clarifying one's personal needs, values, interests, and skills; this is very similar to the self-reflection and self-clarity approach of hope-action theory (Niles et al., 2021). Smith's next circle is "Be well," which clearly aligns with the well-being factor of the capacity component in career engagement. Next is "Be compassionate," which is focused on relationships and self-care. "Be a contributor" relates to work, volunteer, and caregiving choices and links to the importance of "meaning" on the challenge component in career engagement. Smith also encourages older adults to "Be curious," continuing to engage in both formal and informal learning opportunities. Finally, and closely related to the well-being factor of career engagement, is "Just be," with a focus on leisure, play, joy, and creativity.

Applying Career Engagement

The career engagement model is relevant for all career stages, including retirement. Before Abdul first retired at 60, he'd been feeling a bit overwhelmed by the project he'd been working on in China. It was challenging and under-resourced, with a team lacking some of the needed competencies, communication difficulties between the local workers and the expat managers and professionals, and project delays due to lack of necessary supplies and materials. For the first time in years, he'd found himself missing the comforts of home and was yearning to have closer contact with his family and friends in London. He was in a comfortable place financially and easily able to afford to leave work.

For the first couple of years post-retirement, Abdul managed to find a better balance between his challenge and capacity. Although he was often consulted by colleagues in the field who still valued his breadth and depth of experience, Abdul was grateful to no longer have administrative or supervisory responsibilities. He found it intriguing to book his own travel after having office staff take care of that for him for 30-plus years. He turned booking trips into a game, strategizing how to minimize expenses while maximizing enjoyment from his travels. When travel plans were canceled, he once again upped his challenge by taking on projects in his own home and at his parents' place and helping to finance his brother's restaurant and engaging in management discussions about how to navigate the pandemic.

A year into the lockdown, however, Abdul found himself feeling underutilized and gradually losing his energy and motivation. He realized that he needed a new challenge and a project that brought purpose and meaning back to his life. He considered returning to school, just for fun, until his brother had to close the restaurant, unable to repay the loan Abdul had given him. Although Abdul still had some retirement savings left, his situation felt a bit precarious, and he didn't like the idea of having to worry about money. This tipped the scales for him; the combination of diminished financial resources (capacity, in the career engagement model) and lack of meaning and motivation (challenge) pointed to returning to work as the optimal solution.

Activities

16.1   Six Circles of Life

Abdul had been introduced to Smith's (2014) six circles of life model. Recognizing both strengths and gaps at this stage of his life, Abdul wrote his reflections in his journal.

Six Circles	Personal Reflections
Be who you are: Personal needs, values, interests, and skills	I value financial security, flexibility, and intellectual challenge. I miss working abroad and the expat community.
Be well: Health and wellness choices	I'm grateful for my good health; losing a couple of friends this year has inspired me to live my life to the fullest.
Be compassionate: Relationship choices, both with yourself and others	The timing of me being home for the past year and a half was great to help my parents and my brother's family. Now that my brother has sold the restaurant, he'll be more available to help our mum and dad.
Be a contributor: Work and volunteer choices	I've had several calls from colleagues desperate for my skill set; I think I'm ready to take on another project, in a supporting role this time, though, rather than as the project lead.
Be curious: Informal and formal learning choices	I was getting excited about going back to school; I'll check into part-time options online.
Just be: Leisure, play, creative, and joyful choices	For the next year, I'll alternate my time off between heading home to help my parents and traveling to somewhere fun to visit friends.

Now it's your turn.

Six Circles	Personal Reflections
Be who you are: Personal needs, values, interests, and skills	....
Be well: Health and wellness choices	....
Be compassionate: Relationship choices, both with yourself and others	....
Be a contributor: Work and volunteer choices	....
Be curious: Informal and formal learning choices	....
Just be: Leisure, play, creative, and joyful choices	....

16.2   Retirement Activities Checklist

Complete the following checklist (adapted from Neault, 2012), using the three first columns to identify your present level of time spent doing each of the activities and the last three columns to identify how much time you would spend on each activity in your future ideal vision of retirement.

Here is a sample from Abdul. He checked "N" for never or seldom, "S" for sometimes, and "O" for often (regularly or daily).

Activity	Present			Future		
	N	**S**	**O**	**N**	**S**	**O**
Attending auctions	X			X		
Attending cultural events (e.g., theatre, opera, symphony, ballet)	X					X
Attending groups that share a common interest	X				X	
Attending religious/spiritual activities		X				X
Attending social functions		X				X
Attending sporting events	X				X	
Attending to technical systems (e.g., databases, flow charts)	X			X		
Babysitting/providing childcare	X			X		
Bird watching	X			X		
Building/designing models (e.g., cars, trains, planes, dollhouses)	X					X
Building things		X				X
Camping/spending time in nature	X			X		

Next, in reviewing his checklist, Abdul noted several activities that he was not doing now but would like to do more often in the future:

> Attend more cultural events, belong to a group interested in archaeology, spend more time helping at the mosque, have more time available for family celebrations, rekindle interest in building model trains, and perhaps build a small cottage at some point.

Abdul realized that planning ahead would help him create a more interesting and engaging life the next time he retired!

Now it's your turn.

Complete the following checklist, using the three first columns to identify your present level of time spent doing each of the activities and the last three columns to identify how much time you would spend on each activity in your future ideal vision of retirement. Check "N" for never or seldom, "S" for sometimes, and "O" for often (regularly or daily).

Activity	Present			Future		
	N	S	O	N	S	O
Attending auctions						
Attending cultural events (e.g., theatre, opera, symphony, ballet)						
Attending groups that share a common interest						
Attending religious/spiritual activities						
Attending social functions						
Attending sporting events						
Attending to technical systems (e.g., databases, flow charts)						
Babysitting/providing childcare						
Bird watching						
Building/designing models (e.g., cars, trains, planes, dollhouses)						
Building things						
Camping/spending time in nature						
Caring for animals (e.g., grooming, training, breeding, showing)						
Caring for a home (e.g., cleaning, decorating, organizing)						
Coaching/mentoring						
Collecting (e.g., coins, china, antiques, special books)						
Conducting surveys						
Cooking/baking						
Coordinating events						
Creating arts and crafts (e.g., woodwork, sewing, painting)						
Dining out						
Driving cars, trucks, vans, or buses						
Entertaining friends						
Exercising and keeping physically fit						
Fishing and hunting						
Flower arranging						
Gardening (e.g., flowers, vegetables, herbs, plants)						
Going for walks						
Golfing						
Leading groups						

Activity	Present			Future		
	N	S	O	N	S	O
Listening to music						
Maintaining grass and yard						
Maintaining, repairing, or restoring things						
Managing money, investments, and finances						
Massage						
Meditating						
Participating in political campaigns						
Performing publicly (e.g., music, drama, dance, speaking)						
Playing individual sports for enjoyment						
Playing games (e.g., cards, crosswords, computer)						
Playing musical instruments for enjoyment						
Playing pool						
Reading books/browsing in libraries						
Reading newspapers and magazines						
Repairing cars or equipment						
Researching genealogy						
Selling						
Serving on boards or committees						
Shopping						
Studying astronomy (star gazing)						
Surfing the internet						
Taking day trips (e.g., outings to local attractions)						
Taking photographs						
Traveling						
Visiting family						
Visiting friends						
Volunteering for health-related organizations						
Watching movies (in cinemas)						
Watching TV/videos						
Writing (e.g., letters, journals, articles, memoirs, books)						

Compare current activities to your preferred post-retirement lifestyle. Identify changes to make to be more aligned with your vision. Which activities will you do more of? Which ones do you hope to do less of? Try to identify key themes (i.e., activities that interest you). Record insights and reflections in the box provided.

Adapted from Roberta Neault, *Career Strategies for a Lifetime of Success*, pp. 172–173. Copyright © 2012 by Life Strategies Ltd. Reprinted with permission.

Five Big Ideas

1. **Retiring is a process—and may not be permanent.** Many people contemplate retirement for years in advance. Some have a specific milestone date in mind; others benchmark their plans to a specific financial goal. However, changes within individuals and their complex life contexts result in changes to retirement plans. Continue to monitor your retirement plans and goals, being open to shifting priorities and new possibilities.

2. **Meaning and motivation are important at all stages of life.** Although retirement may signal the end of one formal work relationship, for many individuals work offered structure, purpose, and social relationships. Look for meaningful opportunities and activities that you find motivating, whether at home, with your extended family, in the community, or in another work-related role.

3. **Capacity changes; adjust accordingly.** Individuals make retirement plans based on their capacity at the time, and in the foreseeable future. However, changes in your financial situation, relationships, responsibilities, or health and well-being may require changes to your retirement plans. It's also okay to simply recognize that retirement, as you'd originally imagined it, doesn't fit for you. Continue to make small (or large) adjustments to your plans to optimize your sense of engagement.

4. **Think holistically.** The six circles of life model (Smith, 2014) illustrates the importance of concurrently considering personal characteristics, making healthy lifestyle choices, maintaining relationships, continuing to contribute in a meaningful way, constantly learning, and taking the time to "just be."

5. **Age is a number.** Many people and some organizations link retirement dates to a specific age. Some plan to retire early (e.g., "Freedom 55"), others are eligible for a pension at 65 or 67. In some cases, policies require withdrawals from retirement savings plans to begin at 71. However, not everyone ages in unison. Don't let your chronological age determine your next steps; instead reflect on your goals, ability, and desire to continue working, context, and opportunities. Retire when it's right for you.

References

Bayl-Smith, P. H., & Griffin, B. (2014). Age discrimination in the workplace: Identifying as a late-career worker and its relationship with engagement and intended retirement age. *Journal of Applied Social Psychology, 44*, 588–599. https://doi.org/10.1111/jasp.12251

Hamm, J. M., Heckhausen, J., Shane, J., Infurna, F. J., Lachman, M. E. (2019). Engagement with six major life domains during the transition to retirement: Stability and change for better or worse. *Psychology and Aging, 34*(3), 441–456. http://dx.doi.org/10.1037/pag0000343

Luke, J., McIlveen, P., & Perera, H. N. (2016). A thematic analysis of career adaptability in retirees who return to work. *Frontiers in Psychology, 7*, 193. https://doi.org/10.3389/fpsyg.2016.00193

Luke, J., & Neault, R. A. (2020). Advancing older workers: Motivations, adaptabilities, and ongoing career engagement. *Canadian Journal of Career Development, 19*(1), 48–55. https://cjcd-rcdc.ceric.ca/index.php/cjcd/article/view/24

Matz-Costa, C., Boone James, J., Ludlow, L., Brown, M., Besen, E., & Johnson, C. (2014). The meaning and measurement of productive engagement in later life. *Social Indicators Research, 118*(3), 1293–1314. https://doi.org/10.1007/s11205-013-0469-6

Neault, R. (2012). *Career strategies for a lifetime of success.* Life Strategies.

Niles, S. G., Amundson, N., Neault, R., & Yoon, H. J. (2021). *Career flow and development: Hope in action* (2nd ed.). Cognella.

Ronkainen, N. J., Ryba, T. V., McDougall, M., Tod, D., & Tikkanen, O. (2020). Hobby, career or vocation? Meanings in sports coaching and their implications for recruitment and retention of coaches. *Managing Sport and Leisure*, 1–16. https://doi.org/10.1080/23750472.2020.1803108

Smith, N. (2014). *Retire to the life you love: Practical tools for designing your meaningful future.* Summertime Publishing.

Straughan, P. T., & Tadai. M. E. (2018). Addressing the implementation gap in flexiwork policies: The case of part-time work in Singapore. *Asia Pacific Journal of Human Resources, 56*, 155–174. https://doi.org/10.1111/1744-7941.12126

Wöhrmann, A. M., Fasbender, U., & Deller, J. (2016). Using work values to predict post-retirement work intentions. *The Career Development Quarterly, 64*(2), 98–113. https://doi.org/10.1002/cdq.12044

Figure Credit

CHAPTER SEVENTEEN

Staying Engaged Across All Life Roles

Throughout the preceding 16 chapters, we've taken a glimpse into the lives of different individuals and their families as they've worked toward achieving optimal engagement across various life roles.

IMG. 17.1

In the opening chapter, we met the Gill family who was, like millions of others, trying to find some semblance of normal amidst the backdrop of the COVID-19 pandemic. As subsequent waves emerged, we may be hard-pressed to find a single community not impacted by the pandemic, although the degree of impact will be drastically different and long-term implications are impossible to predict. At the same time, a myriad of other events took place—from Antarctica's longest heatwave and over 27 million acres burned in Australia's devastating bushfires to the final step in the UK's withdrawal from the EU, the resurgence of the Black Lives Matter movement, Canada's heat dome, and

Europe and China's deadly floods. Perhaps now, more than ever, we must all recognize that the context in which we live and work has huge impacts on the decisions we make and our opportunities for optimal engagement.

In Chapter 2 we explored our early thinking and research into the career engagement model. Here we met Tom who had been recently honored by his workplace and then, barely a year later, laid off. It is "nothing personal" his manager said, demonstrating that changes in our work situations can happen suddenly and unexpectedly and, in Tom's case with a new baby, at the worst possible times. Although we used the term *career* broadly, wanting to acknowledge paid and unpaid roles across the life span, our original research and focus was on the paid work role; we recognized that research on engagement at the time (e.g., work, job, employee) seemed too narrow in focus, potentially ignoring the context and life roles beyond the workplace that seemed to contribute in whole, or in part, to the achievement of optimal engagement. As we revisited and reflected on the early stages of our research on the career engagement model, we acknowledged the important foundations that inspired our thinking and examined the limitations that we found in the extant literature. So much of what we'd read or studied seemed insufficient or didn't seem to fit with our personal experiences working with thousands of individuals, both employed and unemployed, across a wide range of industries and organizations. We briefly introduced the two components of the career engagement model—challenge and capacity—and the factors present in each. Motivating work and meaningful opportunities combine to form the challenge component, with these factors emerging in our earliest research and staying stable over the past several years. The capacity component has evolved somewhat, now comprising resources, relationships, workload, well-being, and fit.

In Chapters 3 and 4 we delved deeper into the challenge component using Arthur's story to explore motivating work and Hui-ying's to explore meaningful opportunities. Within motivating work, we discussed both intrinsic and extrinsic motivation, and the more recent research into gamification. We acknowledged that motivation can't really be separated from meaning in optimizing engagement. As demonstrated in Hui-ying's case, doing work that matters is significant and important, and this search for meaning is as unique as our DNA; meaning can be deeply personal.

In the next several chapters, we explored the capacity component and all that it comprises. First, we explored resources, which include tangible items such as money, equipment, and people as well as such intangible items as energy and time. We met Esme and Elosie, who seemed to have all they needed to be optimally engaged until Elosie's accident caused a series of shifts, impacting them both in vastly different ways.

In Chapter 6, we met Sadie, a young Indigenous woman and recent graduate. With her story, we illustrated how the myriad interpersonal relationships that exist at work, at home, and in our communities impact overall engagement as they contribute to, or detract from, our capacity.

Workload was the focus of Chapter 7 as we explored how a couple's "load" shifted in different ways after the birth of their twins and how, in turn, this impacted their engagement. Here, similar to our broad definition of *career*, we used *work* (i.e., work-load) while also recognizing that tasks, activities, and responsibilities outside of a *job* (or any work for pay) contribute to the overall load we carry and, therefore, our available capacity. With Daraja and Jian, we also explored how shifts in either or both challenge and capacity can result in dual states of engagement. As a new mom, Daraja was overwhelmed by all the parenting responsibilities; however, she felt underutilized when reflecting on her professional role as an oncologist.

In Chapter 8, Jacquie's story helped stress the importance of mental and physical well-being when striving for optimal engagement. Here, although we explored the impact of a toxic workplace relationship on well-being, a toxic personal relationship (e.g., an acrimonious divorce) could result in similar outcomes. With worsening mental and physical health statistics, individuals, organizations, and communities mustn't ignore the impact well-being has on engagement.

In Chapter 9 we looked at the last factor comprising the capacity component of the career engagement model: fit. We met Kadeesha, who recently retired from the U.S. Marine Corps. We explored how the notion of "fit" had its roots in 100-plus years of career and vocational guidance, most specifically around trait factor or "matching" theories. From our own roots in career development, we also introduced the importance of work and personal values on overall fit within work and other life roles.

Throughout our exploration of the career engagement model, we demonstrated how each of these factors can be considered in isolation to explore a wide range of scenarios. However, in doing so, the interplay of these factors must not be ignored. As Audre Lorde, an American author, feminist, and civil rights activist once said, "There is no such thing as a single-issue struggle, because we do not live single-issue lives" (Goodreads, n.d.) Take Daraja, our new mom from Chapter 7, and the load she was carrying in mothering twin boys. Taken further, we could have explored Daraja's story from the perspective of her well-being, focusing on factors like hormonal changes post-birth, sleep deprivation, and even mental health challenges brought on by post-partum depression. Similarly, this new family could have been the focus of Chapter 6, as we considered the loss of supportive workplace relationships for Daraja while she was on maternity leave and the importance of relationships with family and friends as she adjusted to motherhood. In fact, each of the vignettes could have been explored in every chapter, helping to demonstrate the interconnectedness of our lives and the communities in which we live and work, and the intersectionality of each individual's identities, roles and responsibilities, and career–life challenges.

Leaving the exploration of the career engagement model and its contributing fac-tors behind, in Part II our goal was to share ideas and strategies for working with career engagement from the perspective of individuals; managers, supervisors, and coaches; and leaders and policymakers. To do this, we introduced three employees of a family-owned furniture business who were navigating through workplace changes precipitated by the COVID-19 pandemic.

To begin, in Chapter 10, we met Sonja who had been with the company for 6 years, starting in sales but moving to IT not long afterward as part of a return-to-work plan following a serious car accident. Although Sonja lived with chronic pain, she finally felt better able to manage that pain while working at home due to the pandemic. For the first time in over 5 years, Sonya felt that she'd been able to achieve optimal engagement; working from home during the pandemic lockdown, with no commute, had given her the flexibility she needed to better manage her well-being, maintain her relationships through effective use of technology, and monitor her workload. These positive shifts to her capacity ensured she was able to meet work and life challenges.

In Chapter 11 we met Marcel, Sonja's manager who, recognizing that managers had a key role in engagement, was trying to attend to his team's post-pandemic needs. For Marcel, balancing the individual needs of his staff while respecting the views of senior leaders wasn't always easy. Marcel knew he had to consider the factors that influenced each member of his team alongside the influence of his whole team overall as components of the broader organizational system. Concurrently, Marcel's middle management role required him to advocate for his team's needs to the organization's leaders while also communicating back to his team what the leaders were saying. All the while, Marcel needed to attend to his own engagement.

Chapter 12 took us up another level in the organizational hierarchy to the leaders, those who set the policies for Marcel and all the workers to follow. It is here we met Misha, the head of HR, who had her own balancing act to consider. In Misha's case, she must look at the broader organization, understanding all the workers and their specific return-to-work goals and considering how those aligned to the reality of the work environment in terms of remote versus onsite work. Misha also had pressure from above as she tried to respect her grandfather, the company founder's, wishes.

Deliberately straying from the two-activity format used for Chapters 1–9, there are more activities in Chapters 10–12. These activities provide opportunities to holistically explore all the career engagement factors from the interconnected perspectives of individual workers, their managers, and the leaders of the organizations within which they work.

In Part III, we began to explore engagement from other perspectives, looking at student, family, community, and retirement engagement through the lens of the career engagement model. This is where we began to more clearly position the *Career* Engagement model as a *Life* Engagement model, recognizing that, although we as the model's developers have always considered *career* as a constellation of all significant life roles and demonstrated this intersectionality throughout the vignettes, most people default to the notion of "paid work" when they think of career.

As we moved beyond a work-related focus, in Chapter 13 we introduced Philippe, a Grade 5 teacher who was striving to create opportunities for his students to achieve optimal engagement. We explored some of the deep history and research on student engagement, acknowledging that our goal was not to further complicate things by introducing yet another dimension of student engagement but, rather, to support teachers and students to honor and recognize how lives outside of school, along with the pressures from stakeholders (e.g., parents, governments), can impact student engagement in a very real way.

In Chapter 14 we met Julio, introducing the concept of family engagement and how this can be especially important within collectivist cultures. Family engagement has also been explored by other researchers, but not through the lens of aligning challenge and capacity that is foundational to our career engagement model. In Julio's case, as an Olympic athlete, his whole family had focused on supporting his dreams, often sacrificing their own; however, amid the family's focus on actualizing the dreams of one of their members, they'd all experienced optimal engagement many times throughout their journey together. Although there can be some resistance to involving significant others in planning for, and examining, engagement, Julio's story as he retired from his all-consuming Olympic career illustrated the complexity and interconnectedness of family systems and their impact on engagement.

In Chapter 15 we introduced another family, this time examining their story through the lens of community engagement. As with student engagement, there's a body of literature on community engagement, viewing it from different lenses, but none focused on aligning challenge and capacity as in the career engagement model. Prior to an unanticipated relocation, Elli-Anne, Jacob, and their three children were contributing members of their community, active in various events, the business association, 4H, and their church. Their community, in turn, contributed to their lives in a myriad of meaningful ways. When the family moved across the country for Jacob's work, they had to find creative ways to return to optimal engagement through establishing meaningful new community connections.

Retirement engagement is another area that others have considered, but not specifically through the lens of aligning challenge and capacity. In Chapter 16, we introduced Abdul who had recently retired; although his 1st year had gone as planned, Abdul's story illustrates how unpredictable life can be and the importance of flexibility and adaptability during retirement as well as in other life stages.

Throughout this guide, we've explored the career engagement model, its components, and factors from several different perspectives. Ultimately, achievement of optimal engagement happens via the dynamic interaction of challenge and capacity. Life and work roles are complex and ever-changing with individual, organizational, and systemic influences surrounding all that we do. Attending to our career engagement is a lifelong endeavor and important across all our life roles and settings. Similar to the butterfly effect from chaos theory—a butterfly flapping its wings in one part of the world could result in a hurricane in another—it is the small things that can have the biggest impact. We encourage you to remain aware of when you are moving out of the zone of engagement, toward feeling overwhelmed or underutilized, and to continuously make small adjustments.

We conclude with two final activities and encourage you to return to this reflection regularly (e.g., monthly, quarterly, annually).

Activities

17.1   What's Working? What's Not? A Life Role Inventory

Life Role/Arena	What's Working?	What's Not?
At Work		
At Home		
In My Community		
As a Learner		

17.2   Optimizing Engagement Across All Life Roles

After completing Exercise 17.1, consider what changes (small or large) will help to sustain what's already working well and to adjust what's not. What action steps can you take today to optimize your engagement across all your life roles?

Big Ideas

Although we've presented five big ideas in each of the preceding chapters, we're known internationally for our 10 tips approach. To conclude, we share "10 Tips for Optimizing Career Engagement Across Life's Roles," from one of our many presentations on the model.

1. **Get clear on all your roles**. From parent and child to worker and student, most people juggle multiple roles. Some roles will be more salient than others, and some will be easier to set aside, even if just temporarily. Identify roles that are your top priority right now and others that could possibly be given a little less of your time.

2. **Consider your overall sense of engagement.** Across life roles and contexts, are you *generally* feeling slightly "off"? Burned out, anxious, and overwhelmed? Chronically bored and underutilized? Excited and energized or completely worn down? Periodically check in with yourself to catch the early warning signs of disengagement.

3. **Recognize when there is too much, or too little, challenge.** Optimal engagement is achieved through the right mix of challenge and capacity—a dynamic interaction. Too much challenge will move you toward being overwhelmed or burned out, too little toward being underutilized and bored. Adjust in the moment, if possible, to avoid moving too far into feeling overwhelmed or underutilized; it's so much easier to make small changes quickly rather than trying to optimize engagement after becoming completely disengaged.

4. **Know what's in your capacity to give, and access external resources.** Each role you are juggling will require things from you: time, attention, specific tasks. Each of these draws on both your individual capacity and the other resources you have access to, impacting your overall ability to face life's challenges. Before you agree to an exciting new project at work, or to take on additional carpooling or eldercare responsibilities at home, be sure you have the capacity to be successful.

5. **Take a holistic approach.** Individuals may be concurrently overwhelmed and underutilized, sometimes within a single life role but more typically across several life roles and responsibilities. It's important to unpack the level of engagement in each role and/or activity to identify needed adjustments overall. It may be possible to reduce the challenge in one role to free up physical, emotional, or even financial capacity to take on more responsibility in another one.

6. **Consider your long-term priorities.** Whether working hard for a promotion, applying to grad school, or saving for your child's tuition, don't lose sight of your hopes and dreams across all your life roles; allocate time and resources to keep them moving forward.

7. **Be specific.** With big-picture priorities in mind, pinpoint changes in challenge and capacity that will help to optimize engagement. Considering each role, and all the associated tasks and activities, identify what could be set aside, delegated, better resourced, or reorganized to facilitate success in your life-enhancing priorities.

8. **Remember, it's not all on you.** Optimizing engagement takes a village! Once you've identified the changes you need to make, reach out to others to help you reduce challenge and build capacity to achieve your goals. Consider asking for support from family members, friends, mentors, coaches, supervisors, managers, community resources, financial advisors; the sources of support are endless.

9. **Understand engagement as an individual experience.** The interplay between capacity and challenge is unique to each person within their specific context—it's dynamic and ever-changing. Monitor your own level of engagement, based on current capacity and life challenges. Avoid unhelpful comparisons with others.

10. **Be kind to yourself.** The stress of trying to be the best—the best parent, spouse, child, employee, community leader—can be overwhelming. Too often we are our own harshest critics, failing to celebrate accomplishments while focusing solely on what hasn't yet been achieved. Recognize that "perfect isn't possible" and accept being the best you can be, across your complex life roles.

References

Goodreads. (n.d.). *Quote by Audre Lorde.* https://www.goodreads.com/quotes/181970-there-is-no-thing-as-a-single-issue-struggle-because-we

Figure Credit

IMG 17.1: Copyright © 2014 Depositphotos/Rawpixel.

INDEX

A

asset mapping, 154

B

BIPOC individuals, 52–53

C

Canadian career development professionals, 15
career
    definition, 4
    development and mental health, 8
    global mobility and work opportunities, 4
    lifelong, 7
    pandemic-related changes, 4–5
    as a personal experience, 8
    planning, 5
career engagement model, 5, 34–35
    activities, 17–18
    application of, 17
    challenges, 19
    dynamic nature of, 19
    employee/work engagement, 11–13
    fit, 16
    flow theory, 13
    holistic and specific nature of, 19
    ideas about, 19
    for individuals, 97–106
    for leaders and policymakers, 123–134
    for managers, supervisors, and coaches,
        107–121
    meaningful opportunities, 15–16
    motivating work, 15–16
    multiple roles, 19
    need-satisfying approach, 12
    notion of scaffolding, 15
    paid and unpaid roles, 14
    relationships, 16
    resources, 16
    well-being, 16
    workload, 16
    zone of engagement, 14–15
color-coded warning system, 14
community engagement, 157–158
    in career engagement, 159–160

    ideas about, 163–164
    mapping resources, 160–161
    optimal, 158
    understanding oneself, 161–163
contexts, 3–5
    activities, 5–7
    ideas about, 7–8
counseling psychology, 13
COVID-19 pandemic, impacts of, 4–5, 125
culture audits, 87–90

D

Drucker, Peter, 45

E

Educational Psychology, 22
engagement across life roles, 175–180
    ideas about, 181–182
    life role inventory, 180
    optimization of, 181
environmental-social system, 125
external/contextual resources, 44
extrinsic motivation, 22, 27–31

F

family engagement, 149–150
    asset mapping, 154
    in career engagement, 151–152
    family visioning, 152–153
    ideas about, 155
family role overload, 66
family visioning, 152–153
fit, 16, 86, 117–118
    activities related to, 87–92
    in career engagement, 86–87
    ideas about, 92–93
    impact on job satisfaction and
        engagement, 86
    person–group fit, 86
    person–job fit, 86
    person–organization fit, 86
    person–supervisor fit, 86

flow theory, 13
Frankl, Viktor, 35

G

Gallup-Healthways Wellbeing Index, 76
gamification, 22–23, 30

H

Holland's trait factor, 86
homeschooling, 5

I

individuals, career engagement model for, 98–106
    disengagement, 105
    exploring opportunities, 102–103
    ideas about, 105–106
    identifying starting point, 103–104
inter-role stress, 66
intra-role stress, 66
intrinsic motivation, 22, 27–31

J

jar of rocks, 68–70
job crafting, 35, 126
job demands-resources theory, 44
job resources, 44
journaling, 81–83
Journal of Management Studies (Bailey), 34

K

Kahn, William, 11
"Know Your Why!" activity, 37–38, 41

L

leaders and policymakers, career engagement
        model for, 123–134
    capacity limits, 131–132
    challenge opportunities, 132
    communicating benefits, 133–134
    equipping leaders/influencers, 131
    establishing baseline, 129–130
    ideas about, 134
    risk of disengagement, 133
    synergies, 127–129
life role inventory, 180

M

managers/supervisors/coaches, career
        engagement model for, 108–121
    health and wellness, 116–117
    ideas about, 120–121
    importance of fit, 117–118
    key influencers, 111–112
    level of challenge and capacity, 118–120
    meaningful opportunities, 110–111
    motivating projects and activities, 110–111
    relationships, 114–115
    resources, 113–114
    workload, 115–116
meaningful opportunities, 15–16, 21, 33–34
    activities, 37–40
    in career engagement model, 34–37
    correlation with work engagement,
        commitment, and job satisfaction, 34
    definition, 34
    ideas about, 40–41
    job crafting, 35
    program crafting, 35
mentors, 52–53
Michael Jr., 37
monitoring career engagement, 99–100
Motivating Self and Others (Ford and Smith), 23
motivating work, 15–16, 21–23
    activities, 24–30
    applying career engagement, 23–24
    cross-cultural research on, 22
    gamification, 22–23
    ideas about, 30–31
    impact of goal-life alignment and thriving
        with social purpose, 23
    implications for employee motivation and
        engagement, 22
    intrinsic and extrinsic motivation, 22, 27–31

N

nonpaid work roles, 66
North American Model, 140

O

occupational choice, 4
organizational leadership, 124–125

P

5P activity, 39–40
person–group fit, 86
person–job fit, 86
person–organization fit, 86
person–supervisor fit, 86

positive psychology, 13
Post-It note, 23
program crafting, 35

R

racial discrimination, 4, 52
relationships, 16
    activities related to, 55–62
    as capacity factor, 52–53
    ideas about, 62
    impact on career engagement, 53–55
    importance of supervisory and coworker, 53
    positive workplace, 52–54
    priority, 55–59
    role of mentors, 52–53
    synergy of, 59–61
resources, 16, 44–45
    effect of lack of, 44
    external/contextual, 44
    ideas about, 50
    interconnectedness of, 45, 50
    job, 44
    mapping, 46–47
    in optimizing career engagement, 45–46
    time and energy as, 45
    weekly life role priorities using, 48–49
retirement engagement, 165–167
    in career engagement, 167–168
    checklist, 170–173
    ideas about, 173–174
    six circles of life model, 168–169
role overload, 66

S

scaffolding, 15
Seeing Systems (Oshry), 108
six circles of life model, 168–169
Society for Industrial and Organizational
        Psychology, 12
student engagement, 139–141
    academic performance and retention, 140
    activities related to, 141–147
    emotional dimension of, 140
    ideas about, 147
    link between career engagement model
        and, 140
    motivational engagement, 140
    multidimensional nature of engagement, 140

supervisors, 53
Sustainable Development Goals (SDGs), 141
systems theory framework of career development
        (STF), 108–109

T

technological advances, 4
ticky contest, 23
time and task management, 70–71
transformational leadership, 124

V

value conflicts, 86
values checklist, 91–92
Vygotsky, Lev, 15

W

well-being, 16, 75–76
    activities related to, 78–83
    big ideas about, 83–84
    in career engagement, 76–78
    interconnectedness of work and mental
        health, 75–76
what's working well and not working well, 79–81,
        100–101, 180
wheel of life or balance wheel of life, 78–79
work, notion of, 4
work–life balance, 75
workload, 16, 65–66
    activities related to, 68–71
    burnout-antithesis approach, 66
    in career engagement model, 67–68
    definition, 66
    dynamic nature of, 72
    ideas about, 71–72
    as job demand, 66
    time and task management, 70–71
work transitions, 4

Z

zone of proximal development (ZPD), 15
Zoom meetings, 5